COOK LIKE A LOCAL IN

FRANCE

COOK LIKE A LOCAL IN
FRANCE

How to Shop, Cook, and Eat
as the French Do

LYNNE MARTIN

&

DEBORAH SCARBOROUGH

THE COUNTRYMAN PRESS

A division of W. W. Norton & Company

Independent Publishers Since 1923

PHOTO CREDITS: Page 1: © Sara0215/Shutterstock.com; 6–7: © Gorodissiky/Shutterstock.com; 8: © martellostudio/Shutterstock.com; 13: © Pierre–Oliver/Shutterstock.com, © Ruth Black/Shutterstock.com; 14: © bellena/Shutterstock.com; 15: © Marina Da/Shutterstock.com; 17: © Lynne Martin; 21: © Okrasyuk/ Shutterstock.com, © bellena/Shutterstock.com; 26–27: © Natalie Von Doninck/Shutterstock.com; 28: © Tatiana Vorona/Shutterstock.com; 33: © Deborah Scarborough; 34: © Stefano Carniccio/Shutterstock.com; 38: © Deborah Scarborough; 40: © Johanna Headley/Shutterstock.com; 42: © cody traxler/Shutterstock.com; 48: © Deborah Scarborough; 52–53: © Yulia Grigoryeva/Shutterstock.com; 54: © Ekatarina Kondratova; 58: © Natalia van Doninck/Shutterstock.com; 66: © Brent Hofacker/Shutterstock.com; 72–73: © Premier Photo/Shutterstock.com; 74: © Istetiana/Shutterstock.com; 82: © Gareth Kirkland/Shutterstock.com; 85: © Istetiana Kndrovatova/Shutterstock.com; 88: © Lynne Martin; 91: © tommaso lizzul/Shuttersock.com; 96: © Annastess/Shutterstock.com; 98–99: © Olga Lutine/Shutterstock.com; 100: © zarzamara/Shutterstock .com; 103: © wideonet/Shutterstock.com; 104: © Jayne Duncan/Shutterstock.com; 108: © Ahanov Michael; 112: © cristinemeg/Shutterstock.com; 115: © Alphonsine Sabine/Shutterstock.com; 116–117: © Oxana Denezhkina/Shutterstock.com; 118: © KKulikov/Shutterstock.com; 121: © Barbara Dudzinska/Shutterstock .com; 124: © the food photographer/Shutterstock.com; 127: © Vladimir Voronchenko/Shutterstock.com; 136–137: © Barbara Dudzinska/Shutterstock.com; 138: © MKB Photography/Shutterstock.com; 145: © Camille Cherry; 153: © MaraZe/Shutterstock.com; 157: © JoAnn Cherry; 158: © JoAnn Cherry; 159: © John Chica/Shutterstock.com; 162: © Olrat/Shutterstock.com; 164–165 © Jozef Sowa/Shutterstock.com; 166: © EQRoy/Shutterstock.com; 171: © fritz16/Shutterstock.com; 174: © Symbiot/Shutterstock.com; 176: © seeshooteatrepeat/Shutterstock.com; 182: © fritz16/Shutterstock.com; 186: © Anna Hoychuk/ Shutterstock.com; 188: © WEERACHAT/Shutterstock.com; 190–191: © Anna Shepulova/Shutterstock .com; 192: © Jason Person/Shutterstock.com; 199: © Dream79/Shutterstock.com; 201: © Brent Hofacker/ Shutterstock.com; 203: © Mik Lev/Shutterstock.com; 205: © Krasnie Lapki/Shutterstock.com; 207: © duchy/Shutterstock.com; 209: © Anna Shepulova/Shutterstock.com; 211: © Jayne Duncan/Shutterstock .com; 213: © Nedim Bajramovic/Shutterstock.com; 216–217: © Foxxy63/Shutterstock.com; 218: © Lilya Kandrashevich/Shutterstock.com; 227: © Aleksei Potov/Shutterstock.com; 232: © twomeerkats/Shutterstock .com; 235: © Helena Zolotuhina/Shutterstock.com; 237: © Magndanatka/Shutterstock.com

For information about permission to reproduce selections from this book, write to
Permissions, The Countryman Press, 500 Fifth Avenue, New York, NY 10110

For information about special discounts for bulk purchases, please contact
W. W. Norton Special Sales at specialsales@wwnorton.com or 800-233-4830

Manufacturing by Versa Press
Book design by Judith Stagnitto Abbate, Abbate Design
Production manager: Devon Zahn

The Countryman Press
www.countrymanpress.com

A division of W. W. Norton & Company, Inc.
500 Fifth Avenue, New York, NY 10110
www.wwnorton.com

978-1-68268-327-9 (pbk.)

10 9 8 7 6 5 4 3 2 1

For food lovers everywhere who want
to shop, cook, and eat as the French do.

CONTENTS

INTRODUCTION

"The only real stumbling block is fear of failure.
In cooking, you've got to have a what-the-hell attitude."

JULIA CHILD

I n 2014 when *Home Sweet Anywhere: How We Sold Our House, Created a New Life, and Saw the World* was published, I was thrilled to see "by Lynne Martin" under the title. People were fascinated with the decision my husband and I made to radically downsize our life into a 10 × 15-foot storage unit and strike out to live abroad in vacation rentals without a home base. It became an immediate bestseller and soon attracted publishing contracts from eight foreign countries. Tim and I reveled in the heady experience of being mini-celebrities for a few weeks. Gayle King wanted us to tell her audience on *CBS This Morning* about the challenges of being home free; financial reporters for *Forbes,* the *Wall Street Journal,* and Yahoo Finance asked us how we kept within our budget; radio listeners and other reporters pried into everything short of our sex life; and almost every interviewer asked us what were the most important challenges of living on the road for years. Luggage restrictions, language barriers, and mysterious TV remotes were all contenders, but those hurdles were a piece of buttery croissant compared with the challenges of figuring out how to feed ourselves in vacation rentals abroad.

For starters, learning how and where to shop for food in each country often proved to be more frustrating than trying to get through Ikea in a hurry. Could I trust the fish from the supermarket in those tidy packages or should I splurge and buy from a proper fishmonger, risking certain derision at my lack of the local language? Was it okay to touch the veggies at the farmers' market, or would that be considered gauche? Why are there four different kinds of checkout lines at France's Carrefour market? How do I tell the spice market guy in Marrakech how much cardamom I want?

These and a million other culinary questions bedeviled me as we moved through the world. It's not only armies that travel on their stomachs but also the Martins. Since we weren't living in hotels, eating out daily as tourists do, but trying to live like locals, producing meals every day was a top priority. Gradually, the inkling of *Cook Like a Local in France* began to simmer. Perhaps other travelers would like to know what I'd learned so they could get right to it and start cooking in their vacation rental digs without having to negotiate a steep and time-consuming learning curve.

I learned by doing, and not all of my kitchen efforts were successful. Once, I cooked with only the microwave for two days in a country farmhouse because I didn't realize that in order to crank up the induction burner I had to put a pot on it.

Living in Paris was the last straw. Here I was in the food capital of the world, and yet I was totally frustrated about cooking. I was unfamiliar with French cuts of meat, shopping protocols, and cheese varieties, and I was terribly intimidated by my slippery grasp of the French language and my inability to decipher the labels or instructions on packaged products. I was spending entirely too much time trying to shop for and create appetizing, exciting meals. I needed help.

Enter longtime friend and brilliant restaurant owner-chef Deborah Scarborough. I met my ebullient, charming pal over a table laden with fabulous hors d'oeuvres that she had created for a holiday party. When I tasted her flaky, buttery, savory chèvre tart, I knew we would be friends forever! In the ensuing years, Deborah and I shared our passion for food and wine, and she generously bestowed her vast knowledge on her enthusiastic but non-pro friend. Deborah had joined Tim and me on several international holidays, and each adventure was more exciting because shopping and cooking together was so much fun for all of us.

Deborah's role as my guru began when I was flailing around in Paris. I was desperate to figure out how to make a meal for new French friends, and I phoned her because I had no oven and one of the two burners in the apartment had suddenly packed it in. The people were coming the next day, and I had lost my temper. I stood there looking at my tiny kitchen and its pitiful single burner hot plate and was close to screaming as I tried to figure out what on earth to do. Before you shed any tears about my plight, though, you should know that the top of the Eiffel Tower was decorating the skyline through my cute little kitchen window!

After consoling me for a few minutes, Deborah instructed me to cowgirl up and make a grocery list. Her recipe was for Hanger Steak (*Onglet*) with Sautéed Mushrooms (*Cèpes*), Cream, and Brandy (see page 149). This dish could be prepared anywhere with a hot burner and a sauté pan, she assured me. She also gave me a recipe for a gorgeous champagne vinaigrette to be served over a spicy arugula salad mix. She then told me to pick up a delicious tarte tatin at a patisserie (bakery) and serve an hors d'oeuvre platter that she devised for me: Figs (*Figues*) with Crumbled Bacon, Chili, and Honey (see page 39), plus some spiced nuts and olives to start the party.

That first SOS from Paris was followed by my cries for help from other parts of France and other countries like Ireland, Italy, Portugal, and Germany. I had either an equipment problem, trouble identifying mystifying ingredients, or no idea how to prepare what I did find. Deborah always had the answer. As a result, Tim and I and our occasional guests dined very well. By the way, you should be aware as you're planning your getaway that if you intend to stay in Europe for more than a month, friends and family may suddenly descend. This is another excellent reason to have your cooking chops up—you'll probably need them!

Five years and many meals later, Tim and I took a break from our travels to stay put for a while in California and enjoy our family. One evening in our cute little rental house just a block from her charming Victorian home, Deborah and I reminisced. We laughed about her helping me avoid many culinary blunders overseas, and we spoke of our devotion to all things French. We realized that there were thousands of hungry Americans wandering around Europe with the same challenges I had experienced, and they deserved rescuing just as much as I did. Thus, over several glasses of Côtes du Rhône, our soupçon of a book idea inflated like a perfect cheese soufflé, and the recipe for *Cook Like a Local in France* was written.

We decided to write a cookbook for people who rent vacation properties in France and for cooks everywhere who want to produce delicious French meals easily. Travelers waste valuable time and money when a meal goes sideways, not to mention the sheer frustration of it. We wanted to give readers a clear understanding of popular French ingredients and tips on how to shop for them. And Deborah's knack for inventing scrumptious dishes would please everyone.

Deborah was so excited during our first conversation about this book that she immediately began scribbling down recipe titles on her napkin. I started shuffling through my memory for stories about our years spent cooking and eating in France and other countries as I opened another bottle of Côtes du Rhône to celebrate our brilliant idea. The very next day we started working on a book proposal.

Cook Like a Local in France hits all the marks we agreed upon that happy night. We'll tell you what you need to know to shop smart in France, how to get along with a French butcher even if your French is as terrible as ours, how to make do with what's on hand, and finally, give you more than fifty surefire recipes to make your meals sing, whether you're in Provence or Peoria.

We'd love to hear about your French cooking results, so please send us comments and photos on Facebook or on our website www.cooklike alocalanywhere.com. Bon appétit!

Chapter 1

FRENCH CULINARY
BASICS

"In France, cooking is a
serious art form and a
national sport."

—

JULIA CHILD

FRANCE AND FOOD:
THE SUBLIME PARTNERSHIP

Food is sacred in France, and for some, dining is almost a religious experience. Most neighborhood streets are punctuated with tiny shops where M. or Mme Shopkeeper preside over their delectable wares. An open-air farmers' market pops up once, twice, or even three times a week in towns all over the country. The French are never far from fresh, irresistible fruits and vegetables, luscious wines, cheese and dairy, meat and fish, and outrageously delicious bread and pastry. Even products in the *supermarché* are lovingly displayed. I always marvel at seeing women, fashionably turned out in that nonchalant but oh-so-perfect French manner, inspecting a peach or plum as if it were a Monet watercolor. This brings me to the French Paradox, a source of irritation for generations of jealous American women. How can French women shop, cook, and eat baguette, foie gras, and duck confit, drink wine every day, and remain maddeningly thin? I maintain that this is not a paradox, it's a bloody miracle!

Deborah and I wanted to solve this mystery, so we asked French friends and expats for their explanation. Our findings, though unscientific, are plausible: In France, croissants, foie grass, duck confit, and irresistible pastries are meant for company and special occasions, not everyday consumption. Also, in the cities most French women walk every day, and in smaller towns they either walk or bike everywhere. Most importantly, they practice moderation in their diets, consuming wine, meat, and butter in small quantities. And the French do not eat on the run. A leisurely two-hour lunch is *ordinaire.* They also put effort into shopping and preparing good food, which are calorie-burning activities. Plus, the French do not snack between meals, and many still smoke to control their appetites, which is the only positive thing I can say about the habit. An emphasis is placed on grass-fed, pasture-raised meats and dairy, and minimally processed grains and foods. All of this helps the French to be healthier and leaner.

The omnipresence of lingerie boutiques and extensive lingerie departments in department stores indicates that French women are more interested in remaining svelte and sexy than they are in indulging their epicurean desires. Those willowy women also eat birdlike portions of France's legendary selections of cheese. This, too, is a natural control, since high quality means that a little goes a long way toward satisfaction. We saw this phenomenon repeated in many different ways during our time in France. After we had lived for several weeks in the non-touristy 15th arrondissement in Paris, M. Trudeau, who owned a tiny cheese store (Mémoire de Fromage) tucked into a space no more than twelve feet wide and perhaps twice as deep, began to smile warmly when we entered his shop. His tempting wares were beautifully displayed in sparkling white and chrome cases, kept at the perfect temperature for each variety. He, too, was immaculate in his long white apron and crisp blue checked shirt.

On one occasion, when we were going to entertain friends for dinner, I asked him for some Brillat-Savarin and gestured toward an arrangement of the buttery-colored cheese with the white bloomy rind. He asked me at what time I would serve the cheese. I said around 9 p.m.

He reached into the case and examined several pieces of the cheese, plucked a massive black-handled knife from its perch, and then deftly separated a perfect portion of cheese and wrapped it in brown paper.

That evening, I removed the cheese from its wrapper about two hours before I planned to serve it, just as he instructed. The goal with wonderfully runny French cheese is to present it at exactly the time when it begins to ooze from its rind. Remarkably, at almost the stroke of nine, the buttery inside of the Brillat-Savarin started to seep its velvety goodness onto the plate! As that smooth, rich flavor melted in my mouth, I realized once again that a little bite satisfied me completely. Who knows, maybe I'd get to be like one of those willowy French women. Now, this tells you just how serious the French are about their ingredients. Believe me, their devotion to quality edibles will soon begin to make you rethink your relationship with food!

TO CART OR NOT TO CART

There are at least 20 supermarket chains in France, most of which carry the staples you'll need. The quality of meat, produce, and dairy is very good in these stores, but you'll have much more fun shopping your local farmers' market and specialty shops, plus you'll get even better quality. And what's the best way to transport all those goodies you find?

The wheeled shopping cart that I swore I'd never use became my favorite accessory almost everywhere we lived. It was much more critical than an Hermès scarf, believe me. A week into our first month-long stay in France, we came panting into the apartment lugging heavy bags of food supplies that we'd hauled four long uphill blocks from local shops and the farmers' market. As we dumped the bags and flopped into our chairs, Tim declared that the next day we were going to the major retail store Monoprix to buy one of those carts that everyone seemed to be hauling around. Since then, we've purchased similar trolleys in every country we've called home. For around $20, it's just about the best travel tool you can buy if you're planning to cook and eat at home.

WHAT'S IN A SIGN?

Almost anywhere in France, we find ourselves slavering at the impossibly gorgeous offerings in the windows of the patisseries. There are flaky tarts filled with perfect fruit and brushed with a shimmering glaze; there are delicate petit fours in whimsical shapes and magical flavors. The crisp, melt-in-your-mouth croissants are so delicious that it doesn't matter if everything within three feet of you will be covered in a blizzard of buttery flakes. The French linger at tiny sidewalk café tables, chatting and people-watching, while enjoying their coffee or wine, macarons, and tartines (open-faced sandwiches). Joining them for a café au lait is always part of our daily ritual.

Clear-eyed fresh fish resting on beds of ice on the sidewalk outside the fishmonger's store are fascinating. And we can't help stopping to look at the cheese, sausage, and pâté that vendors have artfully arranged in their windows. Middle Eastern shops tempt us with dates, figs, nuts, exotic spices, and imported delicacies. Mom-and-pop fruit and vegetable stands command our attention, too, as their displays of near-perfect produce and herbs urge us to pick them up, take them home, and do something scrumptious with them.

Usually more than a few of these delights find their way into our shopping bag, even when we are just out for a walk!

As you explore your new neighborhood, look at the sign associated with each shop. When you enter, remember to say "Bonjour." If you don't know the shopping and paying procedures observed in that particular store, watch other customers for a few minutes until you get the hang of it. Then have fun choosing your supplies.

When you take your first stroll in a neighborhood, be on the look-out for the following types of shops.

Boucherie (**butcher**): For meats and poultry.

Boulangerie (**bakery**): For bread.

Cave à Vins (**wine cellar**): An essential stop; if you love wine, make friends with your local *vendeur de vin*—you may get a liberal libation education.

Charcuterie (**delicatessen**): For dried or cured meats and gorgeous pâtés.

Épicerie (**grocery store**): Like a corner market; think an upscale 7-Eleven.

Fromagerie (**cheese shop**): What else can we say?

Marché de Fermiers (**farmers' markets**): The farmers' markets through-out France are astonishing. The array of fresh vegetables and fruits, meats, poultry, fish, and cheeses will thrill your foodie's heart. The vendors are generally very attentive and kind to non-French speak-ers. Not only are the products beautiful, but they are also signifi-cantly less expensive than what's available in stores. Many also have

street market sections where you can find fun, inexpensive clothes, socks, batteries, toys, and lots of other things. Look online for the days and times when the market comes to your area.

Pâtisserie (**pastry shop**): For spectacular desserts and sweet treats.

Picard: This is a chain of stores throughout France that sells only frozen foods. It offers superb quality and an amazing variety of French classics. You must stop in, if just to browse. This isn't your Safeway's frozen food section! We keep hoping that someone will be smart enough to bring this chain to the United States.

Primeursor (**fresh produce**): You'll see fruits and vegetables you've never seen before.

Rôtisserie (**cooked meat shop**): Here you can grab a roast chicken for your picnic or a relaxing evening at home. They often sell other prepared foods, ranging from side dishes to entire meals. If you

pick up a roasted chicken, be sure to ask for a portion of the potatoes roasted at the bottom of the pan.

Supermarché (**supermarket**): You can spend hours perusing all the
delights on offer.

Torréfacteur (**coffee merchant**): Stand back, Starbucks, you have met
your match in the grinding wars! These stores sell fresh-ground
coffee from around the planet. You can bring your own pastry, but
many serve their own and even offer light meals. You won't find
one in the smaller villages, but in big towns, they're not hard to
find. The coffee quality is astounding!

Traiteur (**literally "caterer"**): These stores can supply you with everything you could possibly want to serve for special occasions. They
are stand-alone shops or may be found as a section in supermarkets. You can pick up prepared escargot, foie gras, sometimes whole
meals, and make arrangements for party catering, too.

HOW TO SUCCEED
AT THE FRENCH FARMERS' MARKET

The farmers' market is as much a part of life in France as the cafés
and bistros. The produce is so gorgeous that you'll want to take a
still life photo when you bring your bounty home.

Twice a week, late in the evening, trucks arrived in our neighborhood in Paris. Metallic clattering filled the air as workmen inserted
poles into holes in the pavement. They quickly erected frames, from
which individual purveyors would create their canvas booths in the
morning. The next day we'd find a bustling tent city six blocks long
displaying all things edible. Booth after booth of cheese, bread, fish
and poultry, olive oil, flowers, herbs, and fresh, plump fruits and veg-

etables tempted us. The chaos seemed impenetrable and intimidating. Fishmongers with bloody aprons shouted out their specialties, while produce vendors hawked their wares. There was even a traveling cooking school run by the City of Paris where chefs and students huddled over exquisite concoctions while onlookers enjoyed the lesson.

We observed the action in the market for several sessions before plunging into the fray. We quickly learned that customers wait until recognized by the attendant, who uses some kind of French ESP to keep track of which customer is next. Once the transaction begins, he or she bags the items the client indicates, weighs and tags it, and asks for further instructions. It's a good idea to reconnoiter before your turn, because holding up the procedure is not well received by the vendor or your fellow shoppers. When the order is complete, the worker adds the prices scribbled on a scrap of paper and asks for payment. After a few

days, the vendors began to recognize us, and we felt relaxed enough to try out our abysmal French, which amused them. We were inordinately proud of mastering the procedure, and we'd happily trundle home with our bounty, our little cart bouncing along the sidewalk.

In smaller towns and villages, the weekly farmers' market feels almost like a county fair. In addition to produce, fish, poultry, and meat, sometimes there are live fowl and rabbits. Strolling along the cobblestones with the lilting calls of vendors touting their wares, the scent of flowers and fresh herbs, and the sight of brilliantly colored fruits and vegetables all surrounded by renaissance buildings and churches, is a moment never to forget. It's the essence of French life distilled into a Saturday morning shopping trip. Good restaurants are almost always nearby, and you'll probably see chefs picking out what you might eat for dinner that night if you go out.

Whether you're shopping in a metropolis or a tiny village, here are some things we've learned about farmers' market shopping that you might find useful:

- Go early because the best of everything will disappear fast.
- Bring a basket or a big bag to corral your purchases. A rolling cart is ideal.
- Remember to bring cash!
- Take a reconnaissance lap around the market before you begin making choices.
- Do ask for samples so you won't be stuck with a chunk of cheese you don't love.
- Consider purchasing some still-warm bread, some cheese, and wine for a picnic. The wine vendor will be happy to open the bottle for you.
- Remember that 1 kilo is about 2.2 pounds.

THE SUPERB SUPERMARKET

Get ready for an epicurean coma, and plan for lots of time on your first visit to a French *supermarché*. You'll see products you've only dreamed about. There will be a lot of shelf space allowed for items like duck, mustard, oils, vinegars, and items with names that you'll have to consult your dictionary to decode. Let yourself wander among the wonders, and fill up that little cart (which you've left at the door with everyone else's) with all the goodies you'll need to prepare one of Deborah's creations from this book.

Auchan, Carrefour, and E.Leclerc are the names of the hypermarchés (supermarkets) you'll find throughout France. These retailers are the anchor stores in the big commercial centers, and they are usually closed on Sunday mornings. The smaller chains, such as Intermarché, Grand Frais, Lidl, Aldi, Leader Price, Franprix, and the urban Monoprix, are all typically open until midday on Sundays.

Plan ahead because most stores will be closed by Sunday afternoon. If you've forgotten the wine, cheese, or bread, you'll be out of luck until Monday morning. Lunchtime closures at supermarkets are becoming more rare, although they still exist, especially in rural areas. At first, not being able to shop on Sunday seemed inconvenient, but as we began to acclimate to the French *joie de vivre*, it became our rhythm too. Stocking up for Sunday became part of our pattern, one more step toward our goal of living like the French. There were so many fascinating lessons for us to learn.

For instance, when we attended our first dinner party in France, I was astonished that our hostess worked so hard to entertain us. She presented flaky, hot, dainty hors d'oeuvres, which I knew would have taken hours to prepare, followed by a silky, sublime shrimp bisque. The latter is also an involved recipe. The main course, duck confit, was accompanied by baby potatoes roasted in duck fat, and crisp, lemony haricots verts. The dessert and cheese courses were equally impressive and absolutely delicious. When I described this royal feast to a local friend, she laughed, narrowed her eyes, and informed me that much of that meal must have come from Picard. Everyone she knew served at least one course from Picard, because it makes giving a dinner party a snap.

Of course, I sought out the Picard near me immediately—an easy thing to do, since there's one in almost every neighborhood in the country. It's like stepping into a food lover's igloo! Instead of shelves, there are ranks of open freezers stuffed with hundreds of tantalizing frozen goodies. I spent so much time there on my first visit that it took the rest of the day to thaw out my fingers. Even if you aren't cooking, it's a definite food tourist destination.

HOW TO SHOP
IN A FRENCH GROCERY STORE

When you are a new arrival in any city, everyone else seems to know where he or she is going. And they are always in a hurry. Mindful that most people are impatient when a foreigner holds up their progress, Tim and I developed a survival strategy. When the city bustle is overwhelming, we step out of the crowd, get out of the way, and observe what local people are doing and how they're doing it. In a few minutes, we learn the drill for tasks like buying tickets at the movies, which turnstile to use in the subway, how to queue for the bus, and how to get through the checkout lines in the market. Just taking five minutes to watch the locals can help you go with the flow so that you can avoid feeling frustrated, embarrassed, or discouraged.

The French follow rules carefully, so behaving well can vastly enhance your stay. Here are some tips:

- Whenever you make eye contact or enter a shop it's always appropriate to say "Bonjour." And when you leave, remember to say "Merci."
- Coins are required for shopping carts. Bring a one-euro coin to the supermarket, insert it in the slot, and a cart will be released. When you've finished shopping and return the cart, the coin will be returned.
- If you have a rolling cart for taking your items home, leave it near the front door where you see others. Don't worry, it will be safe.
- Touching the fruits and vegetables is frowned upon in France unless you are putting them in your cart.
- Haggling is unheard of except at flea markets.
- Shouting at your companions across the store or loud talking in restaurants will bring you looks of disdain. Notice how quietly most French people address one another in public and follow suit.

- Bring your own shopping bags, if you have them. Bags are not free in France.
- Make sure you have a chipped credit card.
- If you see a scale with a printer gizmo in the produce section, then you're supposed to weigh the product and stick the label on the bag. Find the picture of the product you are buying on the touchscreen, and the printer will spit out a sticky label. Be sure to label your produce before you get to the checkout or everyone will be really annoyed. Observe how others are handling their produce and follow suit. If you don't see a scale, it means the checker will do it.
- Generally, you will bag your own groceries.
- Do *not* feel stressed when the checker is asking for payment while you're trying to figure out how to get your stuff in the bags. The customers in line will be staring and sighing, which will make you even more nervous. If you make some observations before you shop, you will notice that local people ignore the stares and tapping toes and take their own sweet time with this process. *Relax* and smile!
- Organic grocery stores are trending. To find one in your area, do an internet map search with the word "bio," and you'll be all set. Bio wines are also very easy to find.

PROFESSIONAL TIPS FOR COOKING IN YOUR FRENCH VACATION RENTAL

Read the recipe: This advice sounds elementary, but in recipe testing sessions for this book, Deborah often tapped the page and tsked when I rushed ahead and skipped an important step! So please pour yourself a nice glass of rosé and take a minute to read the whole recipe before you begin prepping your scrumptious meal.

Mise en place (**get your ducks in a row!**): Flapping around the kitchen to dig up a spatula while your eggs are burning around the edges can ruin your day, so get out all the ingredients and equipment you need before you begin creating your masterpiece.

Use a prep bowl: Professional chefs and experienced home chefs alike put out a bowl in their prep area for food scraps as they work. It saves steps and eliminates drips on the way to the trash. If you're renting a farmhouse, the pigs will love you for your offerings.

Lids: Many times you'll find that your rental kitchen doesn't provide proper lids for all the pans, so you'll have to improvise. Try flipping a sauté pan over the one you're cooking with, or use a plate or saucer that's the right size to cover your pan.

Strainer: The lack of this handy tool on vacation can be a serious drag, so you'll have to be creative! A box grater turned on its side makes a good tool for filtering out liquid. A coffee filter poked with holes can do in a pinch. Your own hand makes a dandy egg separator.

Treat your herbs like flowers: Limp herbs are useless. If you trim the stems and put the herbs in a glass of water, and then cover it with a plastic bag, you can store them in the fridge successfully for quite a long time.

Put the lid on your pot when boiling water: This seems obvious, but you'd be surprised how many people don't realize how much faster they'll get results by using a lid. Also, you can rest a wooden spoon across your uncovered pot and when the rising foam hits the spoon, it will simmer down.

No salad spinner?: Here's a better way: Put your freshly washed produce into a clean kitchen towel, collect the corners together, and wave it around until the greens are dry. You'll get the added benefit of a bicep workout!

Put a damp paper or kitchen towel under your cutting board: Your board will be stable and chopping will be less of a task.

Yearning for chocolate chips?: Chocolate chips are an American staple so you may not be able to find them in France. Just break up a chocolate bar and chop it up.

No toaster? No problem!: Drop some butter or olive oil in a pan over medium-high heat. Pop in your bread and fry away. It will be the best toast you've ever had.

Use a salt bowl: It's unlikely that you'll find a fancy salt pig in a rental, so just grab a bowl, pour in some salt, and set it near the stovetop. It will save time and remind you to salt your food.

Please use good quality salt: All salts are not the same. The sad, hard granulated salt that most Americans seem to use does not do justice to the food it seasons. Once you discover the fabulous world of salt out there, you will never be able to go back to the same old salt. We highly recommend investing in some *fleur de sel*. This salt tastes like the sea, and it enhances the flavor of food instead of just making it taste salty.

Taste, taste, taste: Ingredients are not created equally, and what you get at home may not be like what you get in France. Make sure to always adjust seasonings so that the meal you're creating appeals to your tastes.

We have included a weight, measure, and temperature conversion chapter at the end of this book. As you cook, pay particular attention to liquid versus dry ingredients. If not in the United States, also take care to set your temperatures to Celsius not Fahrenheit. The results could be disastrous if you interpret 300°F to be 300°C.

DINING ALFRESCO

France's natural beauty is so alluring that dining alfresco is an essential part of the culture. Every decently sunny day brings people out picnicking in the parks, beside the rivers, and under the trees along country roads. In the summertime, the spacious green meadow below the Eiffel Tower is full of people enjoying their picnics as they watch the French Open on the mammoth TV screen erected below the tower. Lounging there while enjoying Deborah's sensational Chopped Endive, Blue Cheese, Persimmon (*Kaki*), and Walnut Salad (see page 200) and a baguette slathered with a country pâté, all washed down with a crisp rosé, is just about as good as it gets.

Another authentic spot for a Paris picnic is below the Hôtel de Ville (City Hall), on the Seine river. We often gather there with local friends on summer evenings. Everyone brings food to share—salads, pâté, cheese, baguette, olives, sweets, and of course, wine. Watching the sun sink behind Notre Dame as the lights of the city begin to glisten on the Seine, sharing stories and laughter with good friends, are memories I'll always treasure.

Traveling through the country, you'll find no shortage of charming spots to stop and enjoy the view. In every town you're likely to see a welcoming park, and most highways offer rest stops that include picnic tables. If you don't have the time or place to cook, no matter. There is a patisserie, charcuterie, and a wine store in every village so you can assemble a feast wherever you go.

If you are near Dijon in September, don't miss the Fantastic Picnic! You can dine in the middle of vineyards or in a historic chateau. The Fête de la Gastronomie is held nationwide on the fourth weekend of September.

Chapter 2

ENTERTAINING

(Divertissant)

hospitality, *n.*
The virtue which induces us
to feed and lodge certain
persons who are not in need
of food and lodging.

———

AMBROSE BIERCE,
The Devil's Dictionary, 1911

Recipes featured in this chapter:

Pickling Liquid
Pickled Grapes
*Figs (*Figues*) with Crumbled Bacon, Chili, and Honey*
*Oysters (*Huîtres*) with Calvados, Apple Cider, and Brown Butter*
*Crêpes with Pears (*Poires*), Gruyère, and Thyme*
*Roasted Tomato (*Tomate*) Jam*
*Roasted Carrot (*Carotte*) Crudités with Yogurt-Tahini Crème*
Tahini Sauce

ENTERTAINING IN FRANCE—YES, YOU CAN!

We've lived in ten fascinating countries, and because Tim and I will chat up just about any living, breathing person, we usually make some friends in each of our temporary cities. We love to entertain and inviting new friends, both fellow travelers and natives, to our vacation rental gives us a way to get to know them and the country more intimately. Meeting in cafés or restaurants can be fun, but an evening at "home" encourages people to relax and be themselves.

While living in Paris, we once met a charming couple from Italy who happened to be sitting at a café table near us. Since Florence was next on our itinerary, we had lots to talk about. They were in Paris for only a few days and I impulsively invited them to dinner at our apartment. It seemed like a terrific idea when I'd had two or three glasses of wine, but the next morning I was struck with doubt. What had I been thinking? I'd invited these worldly, sophisticated people to a tiny vacation rental that had a limited supply of kitchen equipment, flatware, table linens, serving pieces, and charm. We didn't have enough equipment to serve more than one course. I paced the apartment, a trip of about 20 steps, muttering about my fears. Tim, whose logical brain often rescues me from panic, calmed me down. Then, together, we began to strategize.

When the evening of the party arrived, we served hors d'oeuvres on the wooden cutting board. Since we had only four place settings of everything, we kept the sink filled with hot soapy water and Tim would saunter out to the kitchen after each course, wash and dry everything quickly, and then fill the plates with the next course. Finally, for dessert, we used the owner's truly awful brandy snifters with a French soccer team's logo to serve a berry trifle.

The evening was a great success, especially because Deborah had provided me with her recipe for Pan-Roasted Duck Breast (*Magret de Canard*) with Seared Mirabelle Plums (see page 125). I bought madeleines at the patisserie, and I used them as the base for a berry trifle. I'm happy to report that my invented recipe was so tasty that no one objected to eating it out of those silly-looking brandy snifters!

We had a grand time exchanging stories and discovering how much we had in common. Not once did anyone notice that we were drinking cocktails from jelly glasses and scooping up incredible sautéed foie gras from a kid's Mickey Mouse plate.

Everywhere in our travels, we have found that people are more interested in exchanging travel tales than whether an apartment is kitted out with fine china. Entertaining is all about good conversation, good food, good wine, and sharing stories.

DINNER GUEST PROTOCOL

If you're lucky enough to be invited to a French home for a meal, resist the temptation to bring wine as a gift. Your host has probably spent time choosing precisely the right accompaniment for each course, and he or she may be insulted if you present wine. Instead, consider some exquisite chocolates or flowers.

In France, you'll be served the salad after the main course, followed by the cheese course, and finally dessert. Coffee is served after dessert, as its own course.

Your hands should be on the table, but never your elbows. Pay attention to other diners, and you'll see that their left hands are not in their laps, as is the American custom, but on the table. Also, do not put your napkin in your lap until your host or hostess does so.

Cheese is rarely served as an appetizer. Bread is eaten with dinner, not before. Eat it by tearing off bite-sized pieces, not picking up the whole roll or slice. Butter is not necessary, nor is a bread plate. In France, it is common for people to put their bread on the table beside their plates.

When you are served an aperitif, wait until the host makes a toast before having your first sip. Be sure to make eye contact when you toast the other guests, saying "Santé."

Don't pick up food with your fingers. Use your fork, even with *frites*, unless you're at a fast food joint.

Don't make yourself a nervous wreck trying to remember the rules. If you watch your host and follow along, you'll be just fine. Also, let's face it, your French friends already know you're not French, so they'll excuse your deviation from their customs.

ABOUT CHARCUTERIE—
GRAZING THE FRENCH WAY

If you want to make your cocktail hour easy, just visit your local charcuterie (deli), sample some wares, and pick up some tasty delights. Remember, the French do not serve cheese at the cocktail hour, but only as the course following a meal, so consider how traditional your guests are before presenting a big hunk of cheese on your coffee table.

HOW TO CREATE A BEAUTIFUL
CHARCUTERIE BOARD

Two ounces (60 grams) of protein per person is usually enough. Don't overdo it, unless this offering plus a salad is your whole meal or if you are entertaining a few people for cocktails and charcuterie only.

Deborah suggests that you mix up textures on a platter. You might try a hard *saucisson* (thick, dry-cured sausage), a supple *jambon de Bayonne* (ham), and a soft mousse or a rillettes (similar to pâté, but coarser). A sliced smoked duck breast would be perfect. Then add olives like picholine and/or something crunchy and pickled like cornichons, which are traditional. If you'd like to be more dashing, try making super easy pickled red onion or even pickled plums, persimmons, or grapes (Pickled Grapes, page 37). For color and texture, toss sliced fennel or radicchio leaves with lemon and olive oil.

Serve one or two proteins for a small group of guests. However, if

you've made a lot of new friends and they are all coming for cocktails, then the sky's the limit. Serve charcuterie with sliced bread or some French crackers. Mustard is also a great accompaniment. And a bowl of nuts or olives will probably disappear in a hurry.

You can jazz up your presentation by scattering full-leafed herbs like basil, parsley, or thyme around your gorgeous platter. Although not traditional, they are an attractive, tasty herbal accompaniment.

CHARCUTERIE BOARD

HERE ARE SOME excellent ideas from Deborah for distinctive items you can add to your charcuterie presentation. You can keep them on hand for other uses.

Pickling Liquid

—— MAKES ABOUT 2 CUPS ——

For pickling red onion, shallots, peaches, plums, persimmons, pears, blueberries, cherries, or dried currants—use your imagination.

INGREDIENTS

1 cup (250 ml) vinegar (red wine, champagne, or another mild favorite)
1 cup (250 ml) water
½ cup (100 g) sugar
1 tablespoon (20 g) salt
Suggested spices, if you have them: anise, cinnamon, peppercorns, juniper, rosemary, bay leaf, red pepper flakes

EQUIPMENT

Jar or bowl
Knife for slicing
Measuring cups and spoons
Saucepan
Strainer

Method

1. Slice or cut the items to be pickled and put in a jar or bowl.
2. Heat all ingredients in a small saucepan over medium heat until simmering. Let simmer about 2 minutes and then let cool about 10 minutes.

Continued

3. Strain the liquid and pour over (to cover) whatever is to be pickled.
4. Cover the bowl (with a lid, plastic wrap, or even a plate) and let sit overnight, refrigerated.
5. Use within 1 week.

Variations, Ideas, Suggestions

- We love pickled blueberries poured over goat cheese, on a pork chop, or spooned over a duck breast. If you would like to use a pickled item this way, first add ½ cup more sugar to the pickling liquid and reduce by half over medium heat, until slightly syrupy. Let cool slightly and then pour over the items to be pickled. Spoon some of these blueberries over blue cheese–stuffed Belgian endive.

- You can keep a jar of crispy pickled red onions or shallots in the refrigerator for quite a while, and you'll be so happy to find them there when you have a mad desire to dress up whatever you're cooking. Imagine them on top of grilled chicken or a seared steak, or in a duck crêpe.

NOTE: *Don't put your nose over the pot when heating or reducing pickling liquid to smell the aroma. You'll end up coughing because it's a little potent. You may want to open the windows while you're doing this but believe us, it's worth the effort!*

Pickled Grapes

Serve with pâté and toasts as an hors d'oeuvre.

INGREDIENTS

½ cup (125 ml) red wine vinegar
½ cup (100 g) sugar
1 teaspoon (5 g) salt
¼ teaspoon (2 g) red pepper flakes
1 teaspoon (5 g) mustard seeds
1 small sprig rosemary
1 cup (250 g) red seedless grapes,
   cut in half lengthwise

EQUIPMENT

Jar or small bowl
Measuring cups and spoons
Paring or chef's knife
Slotted spoon
Small saucepan

Method

1. Simmer everything but the grapes in a saucepan on medium until reduced by about half or until the liquid coats the back of a spoon.
2. Let cool to warm. Pour over grapes.
3. Fish out the rosemary and refrigerate until ready to use.

Pairing   Champagne, Pinot Blanc, or Côtes du Rhône

Variations, Ideas, Suggestions   Serve spooned over toasts smeared with pâté or pour over fresh chèvre. These grapes are also wonderful on a pork chop stuffed with Gruyère and fresh sage.

HORS D'OEUVRES

THE PHRASE *hors d'oeuvre* literally means "outside the work," which loosely means outside of the main work of the meal, such as the seated courses. In France, people do not generally fuss much over this course, and sometimes you'll be served merely some nuts and olives with perhaps one more item. Take your pick of the following recipes and be prepared to wow your new French buddies.

Figs (*Figues*) with Crumbled Bacon, Chili, and Honey

There is a short fig season at the beginning of the summer and a longer one in the fall. Figs are delicate, so handle them carefully. Don't buy figs that are leaking or look milky around the stem. If they're green and firm, they aren't ripe. Use them within a couple of days after buying, and keep them at room temperature to avoid losing any of their delicious flavor.

INGREDIENTS

8 fresh figs, cut in half lengthwise
6 ounces (170 grams) bacon or *lardons* (similar to cubes of bacon)
¼ cup (60 ml) honey
¼ cup (60 ml) red wine vinegar
½ teaspoon (4 g) red pepper flakes
1 teaspoon (5 g) chopped fresh thyme

EQUIPMENT

Knife for slicing and chopping
Measuring spoons
Medium sauté pan
Platter or large plate

Method

1. Place figs cut side up on a large plate or platter.
2. Cook bacon in sauté pan over medium-low heat until golden and crispy.
3. Remove bacon. Pour off all but 2 tablespoons (30 ml) of fat (save for another use).
4. Add honey and vinegar to pan and reduce about 2 minutes, until syrupy.
5. Roughly chop the bacon with the pepper flakes.

Continued

6. Drizzle the warm liquid over fig halves and pile bacon-pepper mixture on each fig half.
7. Sprinkle with thyme.
8. Serve to your happy people.

Variations, Ideas, Suggestions If you happen to have some blue cheese in the fridge, try chopping that up with the bacon and pepper flakes and then pile on top of each fig half. If you are using smaller figs, cut off the stem and cut a hash mark in the top of each fig and stuff each fig with the blue cheese, bacon, and pepper flakes.

Oysters (*Huîtres*) with Calvados, Apple Cider, and Brown Butter

—— SERVES 4 ——

This recipe is inspired by the oysters Deborah often begs her great friend Thad Tuck to make for her. He makes them with bourbon, but she changed it up a bit when in France since there was Calvados in the cupboard and no bourbon in sight. You will need an oyster shucker for this recipe. It will be worth it. Buy an inexpensive one if there isn't one in your rental. Do not use a knife to shuck because you might injure yourself.

INGREDIENTS

4 tablespoons (60 ml) butter
1 teaspoon (4 g) salt
¼ cup (60 ml) Calvados
3 tablespoons (45 ml) apple cider
1 teaspoon (5 ml) lemon juice
12 fresh, live oysters
1 pound (½ kg) rock salt

EQUIPMENT

Dish towel
Large baking pan or ovenproof
　platter
Oyster shucker
Small saucepan

Method

1. In a small saucepan, melt the butter and let simmer until golden brown. Immediately add salt, Calvados, apple cider, and lemon juice slowly. It will bubble up so be careful.
2. Place the oysters in a large baking pan on a bed of rock salt. Broil until they start to open (or put in your oven as hot as it will go). They will make small popping noises when they are done, so listen for that.
3. Protecting your hand with a dish towel, place the deep side of the

Continued

oyster in your palm and shuck the oysters, being careful not to lose too much of their juices. (See "How to Shuck an Oyster" below for more instructions.) Place back on the rock salt.

4. Spoon the warm Calvados sauce onto each oyster. Serve immediately. Swoon.

HOW TO SHUCK AN OYSTER

If you're wary about shucking oysters, just know that they are much easier to shuck when they are cooked because the muscle has relaxed. Grab a dish towel, because the cooked oysters will be hot. Place the deep side of the oyster in your dish-towel-covered palm. The hinge side should be near your wrist, not your fingers. Poke your oyster shucker into the hinge and twist back and forth while applying pressure until the top flat shell pops open. Twist as if you are turning a key in a lock. Then slip the blade along the inside of the top shell to loosen the muscle. Don't spill too much of the delicious liquid! Then run the blade between the oyster and the bottom shell to loosen the muscle on that side.

Pairing Muscadet or Calvados; champagne or a crisp Chablis are also great accompaniments.

Crêpes with Pears (*Poires*), Gruyère, and Thyme

—— SERVES 4 ——

Deborah's close friend Pierre brought a big package of crêpes to us when we arrived in Paris for an extended visit. There were so many that Deborah had to dig deep to find ways to use them all. This dish was a favorite at cocktail parties.

INGREDIENTS

4 crêpes (purchased in a package from the market!)
½ cup (120 g) shredded Gruyère
1 tablespoon (15 g) minced thyme
4 tablespoons (60 ml) butter, divided
2 pears, cored and sliced thinly from top to bottom
Sea salt

EQUIPMENT

Knife for slicing, mincing, and cutting
Large sauté pan

Method

1. Prepare this as if you're making a quesadilla. On each crêpe, scatter the cheese and thyme on one half only.

2. In a large sauté pan on medium-high heat, melt 2 tablespoons of the butter until bubbling. Add the pear slices and sauté until lightly caramelized, about 2 minutes on each side. Season with salt. Divide the cooked pears on top of the cheese side of the crêpe. Fold in half and gently press down.

3. In the same sauté pan, on medium heat, melt one tablespoon of the remaining butter until just starting to bubble. Add two of the

Continued

crêpes and cook on one side about one minute, until golden, then flip over and do the same until golden. Repeat this for the other two crêpes.

4. Cut into small wedges and serve.

Pairing These crêpes are fabulous with some ice-cold hard cider or champagne.

Variations, Ideas, Suggestions Trying making some crêpes with the following combinations:

- Duck confit, chèvre, peaches, and thyme. Sauté in duck fat! Oh, my.
- Fresh fig, *jambon de Bayonne* (similar to prosciutto), caramelized shallot, and Brie.
- Roasted asparagus, raclette, and *jambon*.

Roasted Tomato (*Tomate*) Jam

—— MAKES ABOUT 1½ CUPS (350 ML) ——

You'll find that this tomato jam will be a must-have in your refrigerator because it can be used for so many things. Be sure to use ripe tomatoes! Put this out for your cocktail guests with some crusty bread and potted smoked whitefish brandade that you've purchased.

INGREDIENTS

1½ pounds (680 g) small ripe tomatoes, such as cherry, grape, or San Marzano, cut in half lengthwise, or coarsely chopped if they are larger
¼ cup (50 g) brown sugar
½ cup (100 g) sugar
2 tablespoons (30 ml) fresh lime juice
1 tablespoon (15 ml) vinegar (red wine preferred)
1 tablespoon (15 g) freshly grated ginger
1 teaspoon (5 g) salt
½ teaspoon (4 g) *piment d'espelette* or red pepper flakes, if you like things a bit spicier
1 teaspoon (5 g) cumin
¼ teaspoon (1.5 g) cinnamon
Pinch of ground clove
Crusty bread and smoked whitefish brandade, for serving

EQUIPMENT

Grater
Heavy medium saucepan
Knife for chopping
Measuring cups and spoons

Continued

Method

1. Combine all ingredients, except the bread and brandade, in the saucepan and bring to a boil over medium heat.
2. Reduce heat and simmer, occasionally stirring until the mixture has a thick, jam-like consistency. This will take a little more than an hour.
3. Taste and adjust seasoning, and let cool.
4. If it's too thick for your purposes after it has cooled, then add a tablespoon of water and stir. Repeat until it has reached the desired consistency.
5. Will keep refrigerated for about a week.
6. Serve with crusty bread and smoked whitefish brandade as an appetizer.

Pairing   Champagne or Chenin Blanc

Variations, Ideas, Suggestions

- Also excellent with a smear of *fromage blanc* or a slice of hard cheese on your crusty bread.
- Try this tomato jam loosened up a bit with a drizzle of water, swirled in a pan, and then poured over pan-roasted halibut. Fry up some capers and sprinkle over the top.

Roasted Carrot (*Carotte*) Crudités with Yogurt-Tahini Crème

This is a refreshing change from ordinary raw vegetables and dip. Deborah made this up one night when unexpected guests knocked on the door. The refrigerator yielded nothing but some gorgeous multicolored carrots, so she invented this unusual treat on the spot. The guests devoured every one.

INGREDIENTS	EQUIPMENT
20 small farm fresh carrots of various colors, tops attached	Baking sheet
3 tablespoons (45 ml) olive oil	Knife for chopping
3 tablespoons (45 ml) melted butter	Measuring spoons
Sea salt	Vegetable peeler or paring knife
3 tablespoons (45 g) *ras el hanout*, divided (Moroccan spice blend—see *Note* on page 49)	

Method

1. With a vegetable peeler or paring knife, peel the carrots. This is optional as we don't always peel carrots. Cut the carrot greens off, leaving about ½ inch (1.25 cm) of the tops.
2. Finely chop just the leafy part of the carrot tops for garnish (optional). Discard the stem parts.
3. Preheat oven to 450°F (230°C).
4. On a baking sheet, toss the prepared carrots with the olive oil, the melted butter, some sea salt, and 2 tablespoons of the ras el hanout. Arrange in one layer and sprinkle generously with the remaining ras el hanout.

Continued

5. Bake for about 12 minutes, checking for doneness with a fork. They should be just barely fork tender but should give the fork a little resistance. You don't want them to be mushy. Also, you are cooking them in a very hot oven so that they will brown. Color is good! Color adds flavor.

6. Remove the carrots from the oven. Serve warm (not hot) or at room temperature on a large plate or platter with the Yogurt-Tahini Crème for dipping. Sprinkle the carrots with more sea salt and the minced carrot greens, if you wish.

7. Delight your guests!

TIPS: *When arranging the carrots on the baking sheet, have the points meet in the middle since the tips cook faster and the edges of the pan will be hotter. Do not crowd the carrots. They must be in a single layer. If necessary, use two pans. If the carrots are crowded, they will steam instead of roast and the result will be a sad mush with no color.*

Yogurt-Tahini Crème

This crème is so delightful that people will be asking you for the recipe after their first bite.

INGREDIENTS

½ cup (120 ml) full-fat yogurt
½ cup (120 ml) Tahini Sauce
(recipe follows)
Juice from ¼ lemon, preferably
Meyer
1 teaspoon (4 g) *ras el hanout* or
your own spice blend (see *Note*)
½ teaspoon (2 g) finely minced
garlic
1 tablespoon (15 ml) olive oil

EQUIPMENT

Small bowl
Spoon

Method

1. Mix all ingredients together. How easy can it get?

NOTE: Ras el hanout *is a North African spice blend. If you can't find it premixed in the store, that's okay; you can make your own. There is no one way to make it, and families and shops in North Africa create their own blends. Commonly used ingredients include, but are not limited to, nutmeg, allspice, ground ginger, turmeric, fenugreek, paprika, cardamom, cumin, clove, mace, cinnamon, and some kind of chili pepper. If you have a few of these ingredients, mix them together to make your own blend. Last time, in a rental, we mixed cinnamon, cumin, paprika, and clove. It turned out great.*

Tahini Sauce

Once you make tahini sauce, you will want it to become a staple in your refrigerator. Use it to thicken and flavor salad dressings, drizzle over roasted vegetables, or include as an ingredient in dips.

INGREDIENTS

½ cup (120 ml) tahini (ground sesame seed paste sometimes called *tahin purée*)
3–5 tablespoons water (45–75 ml), room temperature
2 cloves garlic, minced into a paste (see *Note*)
3 tablespoons (45 ml) lemon juice
2 tablespoons (30 ml) olive oil
½ teaspoon (3 g) sea salt
Cumin, coriander, or paprika (optional)

EQUIPMENT

Chef's knife
Measuring cups and spoons
Small bowl

Method

1. In a small bowl, stir the tahini and 3 tablespoons water until smooth. At first, it's going to seem as if it's seizing up, but don't worry, it will work like magic when you are finished.
2. Add the garlic paste, lemon juice, olive oil, and salt. Stir until smooth.
3. Add a tiny bit more water if necessary. Purchased tahini can vary in thickness.
4. Add some spices such as cumin, coriander, or paprika if you like.
5. Adjust seasonings as needed—perhaps you would like more lemon or garlic. This sauce will keep up to a week in the refrigerator.

NOTE: *To make garlic paste, peel and finely mince the garlic cloves. Drag the flat side of a chef's knife over the garlic, scraping it across the surface of the cutting board. Pile up the garlic again then repeat a few more times until the garlic is a smooth paste. If you are having trouble making the garlic paste, just chop it very finely. Or, if you're lucky and have a garlic press, use that.*

Variations, Ideas, Suggestions

- Try this recipe with roasted beets, cauliflower, or parsnips. Or mix it up. Just watch your cooking times and temps.
- Try cutting fingerling potatoes in half lengthwise, toss with olive oil and salt, and season with ras el hanout. Roast in a hot oven until golden. Or, since you're in France, why not use duck fat instead of olive oil? To die for!

Chapter 3

—

WINE AND OTHER LIBATIONS

(Vin et Autres Libations)

"Only the first bottle is
expensive."

———

ANTHONY BOURDAIN

Recipes featured in this chapter:

French 75
Lemon Rosemary Simple Syrup
Le Voyageur
Cocktail Fraîcheur

I
n a country whose very name is synonymous with fine wine, the subject has been covered in countless articles and massive tomes. To do the topic justice would require another huge volume dedicated to the delicious fermented juice. Instead, we have compiled a basic framework that you can expand as time and sobriety allow. As a service to our readers, we have been diligent in our efforts to personally lap up as many wines as possible. But we didn't limit ourselves to wine, because wine is not the only libation the country of France is proud of. Its fabled Cognac, Calvados, Armagnac, and cider are the stuff of legends. They are also essential ingredients in Deborah's recipes for swanky cocktails.

THE COCKTAIL HOUR

O
ne summer, Deborah came to Paris while we were there. She rented an apartment near us. Because outside space is a luxury in Paris, we were amazed to discover that her place had a large, plant-

filled terrace with ample seating and tables. This place was screaming for a party.

We popped the bottle of luscious bubbly we'd brought to celebrate her arrival and immediately set about making a guest list. Since Deborah had been in the entertainment business for many years, our list included a distinguished French playwright and one of France's top TV producers, along with a winemaker from Bordeaux and an Italian actor. We contributed a French architect, a Dutch psychologist who lived in our building, and several expat friends.

Preparing for the party was almost as much fun as the event itself. We loved cooking in the well-appointed kitchen and decorating the place with fragrant bouquets of fresh flowers, which are ever-present in great mounds of color at the farmers' markets and florist's shops. The French are devoted to beauty in food, art, nature, and decor, and they have created a cultural atmosphere that allows them to have the time to appreciate it.

Deborah created an exciting charcuterie board with sausage, cheeses, nuts, and rich, creamy pâtés. I was in charge of the fresh figs with bacon, honey, and chili. Although cheese isn't usually served as an hors d'oeuvre in France, we decided that it was so delicious that we'd present it anyway. I noticed that even the most traditional of our guests snapped it up with compliments for the cook.

It was a lovely night, and the tiny lights Tim had strung around the space gave the terrace a soft glow that made everyone look beautiful. The hum of conversation switched languages effortlessly (of course, Tim, Deborah, and I were madly trying to keep up). We nibbled, drank, and laughed for hours, and it was all so very *French* and sophisticated that I kept thinking that I must have been cast in a French film.

The following sections detail what Deborah suggests if you want to host your own cocktail party.

WINE (*Vin*)

Wine. What can we say? So many wines, so little time! France is the place to try as much wine as you can get your hands on. We've suggested pairings for many of the recipes, but you can certainly experiment. In America, we are accustomed to shopping for wines based on their varieties, like Cabernet Sauvignon or Chardonnay, but the French identify their wines by the regions in which they were made, not the grape variety. If you look at the back label of a bottle of French wine, you may or may not find a list of the grapes that were used to create the wine.

Here are some suggestions that might help you in your initial foray into the French world of wine. Your very best friend just might be the guy on the corner who owns the wine shop. Usually, these owners are more than happy to talk wine and educate you. Besides, it's always fun to interact with locals as much as you can. You can also get some brilliant wines at the *supermarché*. You will probably pay between $14 and $17 for a really nice bottle. The supermarkets make deals with the vineyards so you can enjoy the benefit of their negotiations. In theory, a *négociant* simply buys, bottles, and sells wine from outside sources. An *éleveur* "improves" the wine by making it from grapes or freshly crushed juice. Assuming savvy shopping, the result to the consumer can be wine of good value, if for no other reason than that *négociant* wines are generally more lightly regarded than the estate-bottled and single-vineyard wines made on the premises by producers who grow their own grapes. If you're willing to trade the cachet (and the price) of estate-bottled wines and don't insist on top-rank style for everyday drinking, you'll find that *négociant* wines—particularly those

from companies you've learned to trust—can offer a good, character-istic taste of a region and its grapes, without the expense of the more sought-after estate-bottled wines.

Also, be mindful of the year. Good wine from a bad year could be a supermarket ploy! Just like people, vineyards can have good years and bad years. For instance, 2000 was a good year for red Rhônes, while 2001 was not as good. So, if you see a bottle of 2001 red Rhône at an amazingly cheap price, you might want to pass. One of the joys of wine in France is that you can enjoy it in public without being hassled by the constabulary. You can drink it in a city park, along the Seine in the middle of Paris, or out in the countryside. I wouldn't walk down the street with an open bottle, but if you use common sense, you can imbibe almost anywhere.

In the following section, we've listed some of the essential wine regions of France. If you have time, try to explore as many of the appel-lations and smaller regions as you can. They are less touristy and you will probably get more personal attention at the wineries.

BASIC WINE REGIONS OF FRANCE

Alsace: This region, which borders Germany, is where a cool, moist climate produces beautiful, lean, dry white wines. Alsace was once a part of Germany, so the food and culture have a Germanic influence. Look for Riesling, Pinot Gris, Gewürztraminer, and Sylvaner. This is the one area of France where the wines are usu-ally named after their grape variety instead of their place of ori-gin. Alsatian dry and off-dry white wines generally pair well with creamy sauces, scallops, *tartiflette*, foie gras, lobster, roast turkey or goose, and charcuterie as well as French Munster cheese and many washed rind cheeses.

Bordeaux: This region is one of the largest and oldest wine-producing regions of France. It is where you will find wines made from the five great grapes: Cabernet, Merlot, Cabernet Franc, Petit Verdot, and Malbec. You can find bargains here, especially in the outlying appellations (there are 57 appellations in Bordeaux). You can also find some of the most exclusive and expensive wines in the world. You'll enjoy these wines with game or aged beef. Open the wine at least 30 minutes before you're ready to drink it so that it can develop fully.

Bourgogne (Burgundy): This region is home to many costly and sought-after wines because this is where the famous French Pinot Noirs are made. The moderate climate is what fussy Pinot Noir vines crave. Chardonnay is the other grape this area is known for, but this isn't your grandma's Chardonnay. These are made with such finesse and balance that you may not recognize them as such. French Pinots are terrific with salmon, duck and other game birds, mushrooms, roast pork, and also with many types of cheese.

Champagne: Not all sparkling wines from France are called Champagne. Only sparkling wines from the Champagne region of France can be called Champagne. Period. No exceptions. And they are worth it. Champagne is available everywhere, and in France it won't break your budget. So indulge yourself and enjoy feeling *très chic*! In this book, all references to champagne (lowercase) will refer to sparkling wines that are not made in the region of Champagne.

Languedoc-Roussillon: This region tends to be dry, allowing for a longer growing season. Full-bodied wines are the result. These tend to be good finds when you are searching the aisles in the wine shop. They lean toward spicy, which means wines from this region pair well with rustic dishes, wild game, and sausages. We love a full-bodied Corbières. This is also the home of Banyuls, which *Wine Enthusiast Magazine* called the ultimate dessert wine.

Loire: This exquisite region features rolling hills speckled with châteaux. Sauvignon Blanc is grown here to make one of our favorite wines, Sancerre. Vouvray, made from Chenin Blanc, is also a favorite. You can find a lighter version of Cabernet Franc here, as well as Pinot Noir, which is not as pricey as those found in the Bourgogne region. The Muscadet here is delicious. You'll notice that the wines tend to be lighter due to the cooler climate. Saumur-Champigny region wines are medium-bodied. Not only is this wine very easy to drink, but it's also surprisingly affordable. You can enjoy it paired with almost anything, such as chicken or vegetarian meals. And it's phenomenal with goat cheese, which makes sense because chèvre is so plentiful in the Loire Valley that you can find it in vending machines!

Provence: This is the oldest wine-producing region in France. If you are a dry rosé fan, look for rosés from this part of France. You will be delighted. This traditional rosé is not at all sweet. Treat yourself to a Bandol, if you can find one. Drink with shellfish, goat cheese, pâté, roasted beets, charcuterie, sheep milk cheeses, and mushroom tart or quiche.

Rhône: This region is home to 22 grape varieties. The most commonly known red varieties are Syrah and Grenache, and Viognier is perhaps the best known white variety. The sun-drenched hills produce somewhat fruitier and more condensed flavors with a bit of spice. Look for Côtes du Rhône, Côte Rôtie, and the pricier Châteauneuf-du-Pape, which can be a blend of as many as 14 grape varieties as well as beautiful rosés. Generally, Rhône reds match extremely well with braised lamb, grilled meats, wild game, sausages, stews, and roasts.

SPIRITS (*Spiritueux*)

Naturally, most people think of wine as France's most significant contribution to the culinary world, but the French have also been making spirits for hundreds of years. The following are the ones you should sample as you graze and drink your way through the country.

Absinthe: This spirit has a colorful history. It is nicknamed the Green Fairy because it was thought to cause hallucinations and alcoholism. This maceration of fennel, wormwood, and anise was invented in Switzerland. The anise gives absinthe a licorice flavor, and wormwood accounts for its green color. It finally gained acceptance again in 2007, and it is used in absinthe-based cocktails like the *absinthe frappé* or the Sazerac.

Armagnac: This heavier, more flavorful spirit is distilled only once from the same varieties of grapes as Cognac. The region of Armagnac is a much smaller area than Cognac, so it's easy to find smaller producers.

Bénédictine: Also an herbal liqueur, Bénédictine was created by Alexandre le Grand. Any monastic connections are fabrications! It's usually consumed neat, and its rich, peppery, honey-sweet flavor is memorable. The best-known classic Bénédictine drink is the Singapore sling.

Calvados: This is an appellation-controlled apple brandy from the Normandy region in northwest France. It's wonderful in apple-jack-based cocktails, but it's best served as a between-course refresher known as a *trou Normand*.

Chambord: Made from raspberries and gorgeous in bubbly or with vodka.

Chartreuse: Carthusian monks began making Chartreuse in 1737 (using instructions that dated from 1605). It contains 130 different herbs, spices, roots, and barks, and comes in two varieties: green Chartreuse, which is spicy and dry, and yellow Chartreuse, which is softer and sweeter.

Cider: Brittany and Normandy may not have the best climate for growing grapes, but they have the ideal apple-growing climate. Hence these areas produce some of the finest cider you will ever have. Best served cold.

Cointreau: Although this also has a bitter orange taste, its base is a neutral spirit in comparison with Cognac. Its cleaner, light properties make it perfect for cocktails such as sidecars, cosmopolitans, and margaritas.

Cognac: The manufacture of this brandy is regulated by the AOC (Appellation d'Origine Contrôlée, or "protected designation of origin"), so only brandies from the Cognac region of France can be called a Cognac. There are strict rules that demand that Cognac be made in copper pot stills and aged in French oak (for a minimum of two years). When you buy genuine Cognac, try to find smaller producers who have control over the entire process.

Crème de Cassis: Made from blackcurrants and best served at room temperature after dinner or in a cocktail.

Eau-de-Vie: Colorless brandy.

Grand Marnier: This sensational bitter orange liqueur was created in 1880 by Alexandre Marnier-Lapostolle. The liqueur is a required ingredient in the famed Cadillac margarita, but it can also be sipped straight after dinner.

Guignolet: Liquor made from cherries and best served chilled as an aperitif.

Pastis: Anise-flavored aperitif and best served cold with water or ice cubes.

Pernod: Anise-flavored and best served with water and ice.

BEER (*Bière*)

Although France has not been known for its beer in the past, the microbrewery craze that has taken America by storm has now invaded France. And that's a good thing. Even though you could certainly find beautiful beers from all over the world, French beers, in our opinion, were nothing to write home about, except near the Belgian border where hops grow best. But every year it is becoming easier to find good craft French beer, the best being from the north of France, the beer-drinking region par excellence. Beer that you buy in the shops will be slightly less expensive than what you'll find in restaurants.

And let's not forget about cider! There are lots of good artisanal ciders in better *crêperies*, and they are just beginning to pop up on menus in nice cafés. The French observe their rules and to them, cider goes with crêpes and perhaps food from Brittany, but never with quiche Lorraine or coq au vin.

❙❙ COCKTAILS (*Cocktails*)

AFTER A MEMORABLE DAY rejoicing in the wonders of France, what could be better than settling down on your balcony or terrace or sitting comfortably under a tree to enjoy a sensational French cocktail?

French 75

SERVES 2

One of our favorite cocktails. But be careful because they go down very easily!

INGREDIENTS

1 lemon
3 ounces (90 ml) gin
3 ounces (90 ml) Lemon Rosemary Simple Syrup (optional; see page 67)
½ cup (125 ml) champagne

EQUIPMENT

2 tall glasses
Measuring cups and spoons
Zester or paring knife

Method

1. Slice the peel from the lemon with a zester in a long spiral. Cut in half. Juice the lemon.
2. Mix together gin, 2 tablespoons (30 ml) of the lemon juice, simple syrup (if using), and champagne. Pour into two glasses with ice. Garnish with curled lemon peel.
3. Try to drink it slowly. Or not.

Lemon Rosemary Simple Syrup

*Simple syrup is called so because it really is the
easiest thing to make, other than toast.*

INGREDIENTS

1 cup sugar (200 g)
1 cup water (240 ml)
Half of a lemon
1 small sprig of rosemary

EQUIPMENT

Measuring cup
Small pot
Spoon for stirring

Method

1. Add the sugar then the water into a small saucepot. Squeeze the juice from the lemon half into the pot and then toss the depleted half into the pot as well. Add 1 small sprig fresh rosemary.
2. Bring to a simmer, then let cool.
3. Fish out the rosemary and lemon, squeezing the moisture back into the pot.
4. Save in a jar or a small bowl to use in your cocktails or to drizzle over pound cake.

Variations, Ideas, Suggestions

- Use your imagination when making other kinds of simple syrup. Our friend Camille makes some with tea leaves. Other options can include thyme, black pepper, coriander, rose petals, lavender, mint, lemongrass, ginger, basil, grapefruit rind, and . . . the possibilities are endless.
- Drizzle it over cake or ice cream. Sweeten your tea, lemonade, or even your coffee with it. Add it to Chantilly cream. Or invent a fun new cocktail!

Le Voyageur

*This lemony, earthy concoction
will have you begging for another.*

INGREDIENTS

2 juniper berries, crushed
    under the flat side of a knife
1 small lemon wedge
1 sage leaf
2 ounces (60 ml) gin
1 ounce (30 ml) Lillet
1 teaspoon (5 ml) brandy
2 ounces (60 ml) tonic or soda

EQUIPMENT

1 short glass
Measuring cups and spoons
Wooden spoon or muddler

Method

1. In a short glass, muddle the juniper, lemon, and sage leaf with a wooden spoon.
2. Add ice and the gin, Lillet, brandy, and tonic.
3. Stir and enjoy.

Cocktail Fraîcheur

This citrusy delight will brighten spirits anytime.

INGREDIENTS

¼ cucumber, cut into ⅛-inch
(3 mm) slices
1 lemon, cut into ⅛-inch (3 mm)
slices
½ orange, cut into ⅛-inch (3 mm)
slices
1 lime, cut into ⅛-inch (3 mm)
slices
10 mint leaves
8 ounces (240 ml) bourbon, vodka,
or gin
1 tablespoon (15 ml) honey or
Lemon-Rosemary Simple Syrup
(see recipe page 67)
Soda water to taste

EQUIPMENT

Knife for slicing
Measuring cups and spoons
Wooden spoon or muddler

Method

1. In a large pitcher, combine everything but the soda water. Lightly muddle with a wooden spoon. Add ice.

2. Add soda water, one cup at a time, until it has the flavor you want. We tend to like about half soda water and half everything else.

WINE FESTIVALS

Depending on the season, you can find wine festivals all over the country. Look online to see where and when to catch one on your next visit. Here are a few to check out:

Coulommiers Wine and Cheese Fair: This festival celebrates Coulommiers cheese, which is similar to Camembert. There is also a "Brie market" every Sunday in the center of town. The town of Coulommiers is located in the Seine-et-Marne area of France.

The Salon des Grands Vins: This event is held every year at the Carrousel du Louvre, a shopping mall in Paris. Attendees can find out about the world's finest wines with tastings, conferences, exhibitions, and demonstrations. Over 100 châteaux are represented, both those with established names and worthy newcomers.

Les Vinées Tonnerroises: Every year at Easter, the Vinées Tonnerroises in Tonnerre, Burgundy, celebrates wine and winegrowers, mainly from Burgundy, who exhibit a range of regional specialties. There are tastings at the Hôtel-Dieu in Tonnerre where new members from the Confrérie des Foudres Tonnerrois are honored.

Rablay-sur-Layon: This Loire Valley festival offers free theater, music, and singing. The winegrowers of Rablay play an active part in preparing for the event and organize aperitif concerts and a vintage wine tasting area.

Bordeaux Wine Festival: Held over a period of four days in June, Bordeaux celebrates its wines and those of Aquitaine. You can buy a Tasting Pass for the full duration of the festival, which entitles you to a wine glass and book of 11 vouchers for free tastings. It also allows you to visit wine workshops, shows, a giant picnic on the quaysides, and a firework display over the Garonne river on the last day of the festival.

Nuits-Saint-Georges Wine Festival: Every year at the end of March, the Hospices of Nuits-Saint-Georges hold a charity wine auction (Enchères des Vins des Hospices de Nuits-Saint-Georges). This event at Coup d'Oeil in Burgundy is known for the exhibition and tasting of hundreds of wines from all over Burgundy.

Vignerons Indépendants: This is an event held throughout France for independent winemakers. These Salons des Vins occur in October and November. Winegrowers who bottle their own wines host tastings and welcome visitors to their vineyards.

Les 3 Glorieuses: Held in Beaune, Burgundy, this is the oldest traditional wine auction in France. The November event features open house wine tastings, and on Sunday it ends with the world-famous auction in the Hospice de Beaune. For the sportiest tourists, there is a half-marathon race in the vineyards surrounding Beaune. If you can stay an extra day, you can attend the Monday winegrowers' banquet and celebrate the end of the harvest season.

The Flame of Armagnac: This event is held on weekends from November to February in various towns. The harvest is complete, and across three French departments (Landes, Gers, and Lot-et-Garonne) distillation begins. This is the best time to visit Armagnac producers, many of whom open up their cellars to explain how Armagnac is made, offer tastings, and celebrate this age-old tipple (which predates Cognac) with sporting, cultural, and gastronomic events.

Chapter 4

CHEESE, EGGS,
AND DAIRY

(Fromage, Oeufs, et Latier)

"Without butter, without eggs,
there is no reason to
come to France."

———

PAUL BOCUSE

"The way you make an omelet
reveals your character."

———

ANTHONY BOURDAIN

Recipes featured in this chapter:

*Cherry (*Cerise*) Compote*
*Sweet Potato (*Patate Douce*), Sausage (*Saucisse*),*
*and Shallot (*Echalote*) Crustless Quiche*
*Crab (*Crabe*) and Poached Egg Tartine*
*Tarragon Butter (*Beurre d'Estragon*)*
*Anchovy Butter (*Beurre d'Anchois*) and Radishes (*Radis*)*
*Seaweed Butter (*Beurre d'Algues*)*

CHEESE (*Fromage*)

Some experts claim that France now boasts of 275 types of cheese, but others say the number is closer to 500. No matter who is correct, one of Deborah's and my sworn goals is to try to taste as many of them as we possibly can. France (and much of the rest of the world) does not require cheese to be pasteurized (cooked). This allows natural bacteria to do its job and make cheese the whole world craves. Like wine, fine French cheese is controlled by the AOC (Appellation d'Origine Contrôlée), a French food-labeling term that protects the style, ingredients, and origin of a product. Many of Europe's oldest food products are protected by similar designations, such as Italy's DOC (Denominazione di Origine Controllata) and Spain's DO (Denominación de Origen). That means, for example, that if you buy any cheese called Roquefort, it must have been produced in the Roquefort area of France; likewise the famous Comté must have been made only in the Franche-Comté region in eastern France.

Most of France's hard cheeses are best kept in a cool, dark, well-ventilated place, not in the refrigerator. They'll keep better if they are loosely wrapped in paper, not in plastic. Moisture collects between the cheese and the plastic, and it prevents the cheese from breathing correctly.

We once house-sat for friends of ours at their apartment on Butte Montmartre, in Paris. The apartment was in a fabulous 1904 art nouveau building. There was a tiny door next to the outside wall of the kitchen, and the friend who owned the place explained that in many old French buildings there was a *garde manger* like his. Before refrigeration, it was used to keep food; and if people are lucky enough to have one today, it's where they can store their cheese. Of course, there are adorable, expensive decorator creations called "cheese safes" for those poor souls who don't have a *garde manger*.

Following are some of our favorite cheeses from the seemingly infinite kinds available, and suggestions about how to use them. We encourage you to explore and discover unique local artisanal cheeses. Of course, *supermarchés* stock cheeses of all sorts, and what you will find depends on the snootiness of the store. Truth be told, you'll have a better cheese-buying experience in the small shops or farmers' markets. The sellers will be delighted to give you a short cheese lesson and even a taste of their wares.

Fresh Cheese

Fromage Blanc is a fresh, very soft cow's-milk cheese, a cross between yogurt and ricotta. It's made with whole or skimmed milk and cream. Without the cream, it's virtually fat-free, but of course, cream makes it taste better! It's used in desserts, as a spread on bread, and in savory dishes.

Petit-Suisse is made from cow's milk in Pays de Bray. It has a smooth texture and is usually eaten for dessert or breakfast topped with something sweet. It comes in a cylindrical shape in a little plastic tub. You can enjoy it with savory herbs or add it to other ingredients to make a spreadable consistency. It's sold very fresh and should be consumed soon after you buy it.

Soft Cheese

Brie de Meaux and ***Brie de Melun*** are AOC cheeses made from cow's milk. This is the authentic Brie! Since it is not pasteurized, the cheese has a beefy, buttery flavor and a gorgeous golden color. The tender white crust is eaten, and its mild flavor and creamy consistency should please almost anyone who doesn't like strong-tasting cheese.

Brillat-Savarin is made in Pays de Bray. It is a triple cream cow's-milk cheese, extremely soft and creamy. A mature Brillat-Savarin has a white rind with a buttery-white interior. It's a gorgeous treat with champagne, but then what doesn't go with champagne? It's also nice with Viognier.

Camembert is from Normandy. This soft, creamy cheese from cow's milk is probably the most famous French cheese as well as the most imitated. It should be soft but not too runny when you buy it. If it's hard, it's not aged properly. If it's yellow, it's seen better days. To be sure of what you're getting, open the box and press on the cheese. If it's not soft, move on to something else. Eat the rind as well as the cheese. Properly stored it should last a week in the refrigerator.

Carré de l'Est is a soft-ripened cow's-milk cheese with a smoky bacon flavor. It is extremely popular in France and can be found almost everywhere in the country.

Chabichou du Poitou is made in the Poitou, Berry, and Périgord regions of France from goat's milk. Many of these cheeses are sold locally, but since it's made in both raw and pasteurized versions, it can also be found in the United States. The cheeses are shaped like small cylinders and have a wrinkly rind. When it's young, it has a clean, mildly sweet goat flavor; and with age, it becomes more chalky with a nutty taste.

Crottin de Chavignol is made in a village near Sancerre from goat's milk. This is the Loire region's most famous cheese. Its natural rind can range from pale ivory to almost black, and its interior is a soft flaky white. It can be eaten almost anytime during its ripening process and gets more vibrant as it ages. It's marvelous served warm in a chèvre salad and perfect for a cheeseboard.

Munster is made in Alsace-Lorraine from cow's milk and is not at all like the mild American version, which is known as Muenster (notice the slight difference in spelling). The French variety has a much more pungent aroma and an assertive flavor. The rind can be eaten or cut off as you prefer. Although strong, it should never taste acrid. If it does, it's overripe.

St. André, from Villefranche-de-Rouergue, is a triple cream cow's-milk cheese. Its high fat content, enhanced with heavy cream, gives it a gloriously buttery taste. Its powdery rind and decadent center make it seem like Brie to the triple power. Think of this cheese with a soft dessert wine or slathered on a crunchy baguette. Excuse me—I have to leave for France right this minute!

Pont-l'Évêque is made in Pays d'Auge from cow's milk. This is a terrific addition to an after-dinner cheese plate. Eat the orange rind, too. Inside, you'll find a creamy, soft cheese with a strong aroma but a mild flavor.

Vacherin is made in the Haut-Doubs from pasteurized cow's milk. It has a grayish-yellow rind that you'll want to remove. Since it's covered in pine bark, it has a slight resinous note. It's very runny, so it's best served with a spoon. It's considered a rare and luxurious cheese since it's produced only from August 15 through March 31.

Semi-Soft Cheese

Comté is from the Franche-Comté region of eastern France. This firm cow's-milk cheese is made in local village dairies whose methods haven't changed in hundreds of years. It comes either *fruite* (fruity) or *sale* (salty). It's the traditional cheese of fondue and also is used for raclette. Considered one of the most excellent cheeses in the world, a wedge of Comté has a pale yellow interior and a texture that can vary from smooth to hard. The cheese is aged in caves in the area, and on the labels of some Comté you'll see the name of the cave in which it matured.

Époisses is made in Semur-en-Auxois, Burgundy, from cow's milk. It's semi-soft with an orange rind and a white center that's almost crumbly. The cheese under the skin is soft. It's wonderful with red wine.

Mâconnais is made in Mâcon, Burgundy, from goat's milk, cow's milk, or a combination of the two. It's shaped like a cone and is cream colored, but as it ripens it may turn blue. It's creamy, but as it ages it becomes harder and saltier. Try it with a light red wine like a Beaujolais or a light white like Chablis. This cheese was certified AOC in 2005.

Morbier is made in Franche-Comté from cow's milk. It's a semi-soft, ivory-colored cheese that is easy to spot because of its layer of black ash in the middle. The traditional line of ash is now just decoration and has no taste. The cheese is strongly scented and has a yellow rind.

Blue Cheese

Bleu de Bresse is made in Bresse from cow's milk. It is rich, creamy, and deliciously blue. Its rind is soft and edible like Brie.

Fourme d'Ambert is a cow's-milk cheese made in Monts du Forez. It is one of the oldest cheeses in France, and legend has it that the Druids and the Gauls were making it in their time. It is the mildest of the blues and is great in salads and on cheese boards.

Roquefort is made in Roquefort-sur-Soulzon from unpasteurized sheep's milk. This soft, crumbly cheese was reportedly a favorite of the emperor Charlemagne. In France, Roquefort is called the cheese of kings and popes. It is protected by AOC and is aged for five months. Almost anything savory can benefit from a little Roquefort!

Semi-Firm

Beaufort, made of unpasteurized cow's milk, comes from the same region in the Alps as the Tomme de Savoie. It has a distinct aroma of earth and grass. It's yellow, with a smooth and creamy texture, and it is a favorite cheese for fondue because it melts quickly. It's terrific with fish.

Tomme de Savoie is made in the valley of Savoie in the French Alps. The word *tomme* means a small wheel of cheese, so the name of this cheese really means "cheese from Savoie." It's made from skimmed cow's milk, and it tastes as earthy and rustic as the caves where it is aged. It's beautiful with walnuts, or try it in a salad with sharp arugula.

Hard

Abondance is from the Haute-Savoie region in the Rhône-Alpes. It is produced from the milk of the Abondance breed of cattle, and this cheese has been AOC designated since 1990. Its strong smell and intensely fruity, buttery flavor make it unique. Its crust and the layer beneath should be removed before eating. It melts well and can be a great addition to a salad.

Cantal is made in Auvergne. It is made from cow's milk, and it is medium-firm and slightly crumbly. Some say its flavor is reminiscent of a cheddar. You can buy *jeune* (young) or *entre deux* (between two), which is the more aged, stronger-tasting variety.

Mimolette is raw cow's milk cheese with a crunchy yet melt-in-your-mouth texture. It has a bright orange color and a thicker rind, which you should discard. The flavors are well developed at one to two years with hints of toasted nuts, butterscotch, and bacon. It pairs well with Pinot Noir or Grenache.

How to Present the Cheese Course

If you're following French protocol, the cheese course should be served before the dessert. If you want to skip the dessert, you can opt to serve the cheese with fruit and honey. Or you could combine your salad and cheese course by serving a small wedge of cheese as an accompaniment to your light, simple salad.

For a full cheese course, choose between two and four cheeses that you enjoy. For instance, you could present a blue, a fresh chèvre, an aged soft cheese, and/or a medium-to-hard cheese. Place the cheeses on a board, a cake plate, a platter, or whatever you can find. Add a light accompaniment with each cheese, such as fresh fig with blue cheeses, or apple slices with aged soft cheese. Be sure to serve the cheeses at room temperature so you can experience their full flavor. If you don't want to do a full cheese course, you can buy one cheese and put a small wedge of it on a small plate for each guest. Try blue cheese drizzled with honey, toasted walnuts, and fresh thyme.

Cheese is rarely served as an appetizer. But rules are made to be broken, so do what makes you happy!

EGGS (*Oeufs*)

The French, ever mindful of good quality food, have borrowed a free-range system from neighboring Germany in which hens are allowed to leave the barn and enjoy runs alongside the chicken house. In 2016, 70 percent of the eggs eaten by the French were produced in this kind of improved system, and there's talk of making all eggs free-range by 2022.

Writing this book prompted us to find the answer to a question that has bothered me for decades: In France and other countries where I've lived, almost everyone keeps their fresh eggs right on the counter. In fact, I have two antique wire baskets that were designed for that purpose. In America, everyone I know keeps eggs in the refrigerator. Why is that? Because our refrigerators are bigger? Because our government rules demand it? Because French chickens, like French people, are just naturally more elegant? Are you curious beyond belief right now? Let me help you out. In America, our commercial eggs are washed clean of their natural cuticle outside the shell. In France, the cuticle remains and so the egg is protected from outside elements. An unwashed egg can last for up to a month on the counter, whereas a washed egg should only be unrefrigerated for one day. Whew! One more of life's mysteries solved. Now, if I can just find out why my omelets are never quite as tender as Deborah's, I'll be a happy egghead.

BUTTER (*Beurre*)

I love to write, cook, and eat. That said, do you have any idea what a sacrifice I am making for you readers? Every day I am forced to think, read about, look at photos of, and write about *food*. So let's just say that the thought of watching the beckoning interior crevices of a fragrant, hot, crunchy baguette embrace the sweet, slightly sour, silken dribble of melting French butter almost makes me weep with desire.

French butter is different from any other on earth. There are literally thousands of butters to be found all over the country, and each has its own particular characteristics. The high quality of the cream makes the difference. Also, the cows' diet makes an indelible imprint on the taste of the final product.

For instance, Isigny butter is produced in a small seaside village in Normandy. The *terroir* (earth) is advantageous, the climate is mild, and the fields are near salt marshes, so the grass that the cattle graze on is enriched with iodine and other minerals. That sweet, nutty, salty spread on a piece of warm French bread is worth every calorie.

Jean-Yves Bordier, the creator of Bordier butter, was the first to combine the flavor of seaweed and the plant's lovely red, green, and black bits into butter. It's particularly tasty paired with fish and seafood, and it can add a surprise finish to rare red meat. David Lebovitz, the celebrated food writer, admits that he refuses to let any other butter other than Bordier cross his lips! If you can't get Bordier butter, don't worry. Deborah has a recipe that you can use to make your own: Seaweed Butter (*Beurre d'Algues*) on page 95.

Like wine and cheese, high-end butter in France must meet certain standards to qualify for their AOC (the controlled designation of area) label. This is the French certification granted to certain products that correspond to a specific geographical location or origin. This certification assures that the product possesses certain qualities because of the *terroir* or because it is made using traditional methods or has a certain reputation.

Although the big-name butters from France are appreciated worldwide, many local farmers make their own sublime renditions and bring them to farmers' markets. And they will almost certainly offer you a taste. Like eggs, butter is best kept unrefrigerated. There are many ingenious butter keepers that supply a little moisture and provide protection from light.

We always beg Deborah's friend Nadine, who lives in Brittany, to bring butter when she comes to visit the United States. It travels very well. Shhhhhh—don't mention this to the customs official.

Although French butters are out of this world on their own, sometimes we want to change it up and use a compound butter (butter plus other ingredients). These can take a sensational butter to the next level. Compound butters won't be super smooth without the assistance of a food processor, but with a little elbow grease, you can make a lovely compound butter or two that will still taste divine. Always start with unsalted butter.

YOGURT (*Yaourt*)

Remember the part about French women and their downright magical ability to eat all that gorgeous food and remain slender? Well, here's another one of their sneaky little tricks—they eat *a lot* of yogurt! Even though French yogurt is higher in fat than American yogurt, it is also much tastier and has plenty of calcium, which maintains bone density and muscle mass while encouraging fat loss. French people eat yogurt for breakfast, snacks, and sometimes for dessert. Once you taste the real thing, you'll understand why! When you go to the *supermarché,* you'll discover so many choices that you can try a different one every day and never run out of exciting new tastes.

Yogurt makes a great at-home breakfast mixed with fruit and local honey. Enjoy it with a big slice of bread topped with the famous French butters we've been telling you about, and you'll be all set for the day.

The yogurt is luscious on its own, but here are some of Deborah's ideas to enhance your meal. Try various combinations:

- Chopped fresh fruit, almost any fruit
- Roasted nuts or seeds
- Local honey
- Dried fruit
- Granola
- Jam or compote
- Toasted coconut
- Cucumber and mint
- Deborah's personal favorite combination is fresh blueberries, honey, fresh mint, and an orange quarter squeezed over the top.

Cherry (*Cerise*) Compote

—— MAKES ABOUT 1½ CUPS (360 ML) ——

This cherry compote is a versatile recipe that you can make ahead. Try it on your morning yogurt (the little shot of wine will start your day right) or on crêpes, pound cake, a cheese plate, or over ice cream. The only fiddly part of this preparation is pitting the cherries. Your rental most likely will not have a cherry/olive pitter, so you'll have to improvise. Place an empty wine or beer bottle in a bowl to catch the juice. Put a cherry on top and use a chopstick, straw, skewer, or a pastry tip to push the pit into the bottle. You now have a pitted cherry. Keep going until you have enough. If you're traveling with kids, this is a nice little chore to keep them busy while you sip your afternoon champagne.

INGREDIENTS

1 pound (450 g) fresh cherries, pits removed, barely chopped
¼ cup (60 ml) red wine
2 tablespoons (30 ml) Cognac or Calvados
2 tablespoons (30 ml) orange juice
¼ cup (50 g) sugar
2 tablespoons (30 ml) honey
1 teaspoon (3 g) orange zest
Pinch of salt

EQUIPMENT

Jar with lid
Measuring cups and spoons
Medium pot

Method

1. Put all ingredients in a pot and simmer until reduced, about 20 minutes. The liquid should be syrupy. If it's not, continue simmering and check the consistency every 10 minutes. Then let cool.
2. Store in a jar or a small bowl, covered, and enjoy all that goodness any time you like.

EGGS (*Oeufs*)

ONCE YOU HAVE TRIED Deborah's crustless quiche, you'll never make those soggy overnight breakfast casseroles again. I never thought of crab for breakfast before in my life, but since I was introduced to a crab tartine it has become one of my most vivid cravings.

Sweet Potato (*Patate Douce*), Sausage (*Saucisse*), and Shallot (*Echalote*) Crustless Quiche

—— SERVES 6 ——

This is the best quiche ratio of egg to cream. You can make it with a crust if you have the time and inclination, but Deborah usually makes it crustless. If you do decide to use a crust, par bake it before filling with the quiche mixture. It can be made in a quiche pan, a pie plate, a cast-iron pan (her favorite), muffin tins, or individual soufflé dishes.

INGREDIENTS

FILLING
2 chorizo sausages (raw), removed from casing
6 shallots, cut in 6 to 8 pieces each
Butter (if necessary)
1 sweet potato, cut into 1/4-inch (6 mm) dice
Salt
Pepper

EQUIPMENT
Knife
Medium sauté pan or cast-iron pan (preferred)
Mixing bowl
Slotted spoon
Whisk (or fork)

Continued

EGG MIXTURE

The rule of thumb is ½ cup (120 ml) half-and-half or cream for each egg. You can feel free to use more of each if your cooking vessel is larger. Make sure to adjust your seasonings.

3 large farm fresh eggs
1½ cups (350 ml) cream or
    half-and-half

Pinch of nutmeg
Pinch of coriander (optional)
½ teaspoon (2.5 g) salt
Pepper
¾ cup (170 g) grated Comté or
    Cantal Jeune cheese (or another
    mild-medium cheese)

Method

Filling

1. In a medium sauté pan, cook the *saucisse* chorizo on medium heat until crumbly and cooked through. Remove chorizo from pan with slotted spoon.

2. In the same pan, using the grease from the chorizo, sauté the shallots on medium-low until nicely caramelized. Remove from pan with a slotted spoon.

3. Again in the same pan, add some butter if most of the chorizo grease is gone, and sauté the sweet potatoes until golden and cooked through. (You can also cook these, tossed in butter, salt, and pepper, in an oven at 350°F (180°C) in a single layer on a baking sheet.) Season with salt and pepper and set aside.

4. Mix the chorizo, shallots, and sweet potatoes together and place in your greased baking pan of choice. Don't overfill the pan. Depending on the sizes of the chorizo and sweet potato, you may have too much filling mixture. It should not fill more than one-quarter of your baking pan. Use the remaining mixture for another use, such as in scrambled eggs or a delicious tartine.

Egg mixture

1. Preheat oven to 300°F (150°C).

2. Whisk the eggs, cream, nutmeg, coriander, salt, and pepper together thoroughly.

3. Pour the egg mixture over the filling ingredients in the pan, sprinkle with cheese, and bake until no longer wiggly in the middle. Do not turn up the heat and do not overcook. This will turn out silky and custardy if cooked properly. If not, the eggs may scramble a bit. Don't worry if this happens because it will still be delicious.

Variations, Ideas, Suggestions A quiche is a super way to use up whatever leftover ingredients you have in your refrigerator, such as tomatoes, herbs, garlic, onions, or spinach. Here are some combinations to try:

- Roasted tomato, basil, and chèvre
- *Lardons* and asparagus
- Mushroom and Gruyère
- Caramelized garlic, spinach, and Cantal cheese
- Use your imagination!

Crab (*Crabe*) and Poached Egg Tartine

—— SERVES 4 ——

If you bought too much crab and mâche
(lamb's lettuce), use them for breakfast.

INGREDIENTS

4 eggs
Four 1-inch-thick slices of good
  quality brown bread
4 tablespoons (60 ml) butter, plus
  extra for toast
1 cup (250 ml) cooked fresh crab
  meat
1½ cups (375 ml) *mâche*
¼ lemon for squeezing, or grapefruit juice
Sea salt

EQUIPMENT

Medium sauté pan
Slotted spoon
Small sauté pan or saucepot

Method

1. In the small pan, poach the eggs slowly. Do not overcook.
2. While the eggs are cooking, toast the bread slices in a pan on medium heat with a bit of butter on each side. Place on four plates.
3. Add 4 tablespoons butter to the bread-toasting pan on medium heat and let brown. Turn off heat.
4. Barely warm the crab meat in the brown butter and spoon on top of the toasts.
5. Fish out the poached egg with a slotted spoon and place a well-drained poached egg on top of the crab. Drizzle with the browned butter from the pan. Place some *mâche* on top and squeeze a bit of lemon) on top.
6. Sprinkle with sea salt. Devour!

BUTTER (*Beurre*)

IF YOU THINK that there are just two kinds of butter, salted and unsalted, let us open the door to whole new world of flavors. Deborah showed us how to elevate butter into a flavor enhancer you'll want to keep in your refrigerator all the time.

Tarragon Butter (*Beurre d'Estragon*)

—— MAKES ABOUT ½ CUP (120 ML) ——

This will take salmon, poultry, and steak to a new level.

INGREDIENTS

1 tablespoon (15 g) very finely
  minced tarragon
3–4 drops fresh lemon juice
Sea salt
8 tablespoons (120 ml) unsalted
  butter, softened

EQUIPMENT

Bowl
Fork
Knife for mincing

Method

1. With a fork, mix and mash the tarragon, lemon, salt, and butter together until smooth.
2. Taste and add more salt or lemon if necessary.
3. Refrigerate until ready to use.

Anchovy Butter (*Beurre d'Anchois*) and Radishes (*Radis*)

This is a French classic, with the addition of the anchovies. The butter is also amazing slathered on a steak or tossed with roasted potatoes.

INGREDIENTS

1 anchovy, finely minced, or
   1 tablespoon (5 ml) anchovy
   paste
8 tablespoons (120 ml) unsalted
   butter, softened
A few drops of lemon juice
12 farm fresh radishes, cleaned with
   a little bit of the green tops still
   attached
Sea salt

EQUIPMENT

Knife for mincing and mashing
Bowl
Fork for mixing and mashing

Method

1. With a fork or the edge of a chef's knife, mash the minced anchovy until it resembles a paste.
2. Mix and mash with the butter and lemon juice until blended and smooth.
3. Refrigerate until ready to use. Serve softened with fresh radishes.
4. Or, dip radishes in the softened butter, sprinkle with sea salt and refrigerate until ready to eat.

Seaweed Butter (*Beurre d'Algues*)

———— MAKES ABOUT ½ CUP (120 ML) ————

Wonderful on shellfish, tossed with rice, or melted and drizzled hot over raw oysters. Try with roasted mushrooms or slathered on crusty bread.

INGREDIENTS

1 tablespoon (15 ml) very finely
   minced dulse
3–4 drops fresh lemon juice
Sea salt to taste
8 tablespoons (120 ml) unsalted
   butter, softened

EQUIPMENT

Baking pan
Bowl
Fork
Knife for mincing
Sauté pan, if necessary

Method

1. Preheat oven to 225°F (110°C). Roast the dulse in a single layer on a baking pan until dry and crisp. Let cool a bit, then finely mince or crumble. If it's already dry, mince or crumble it and then toast lightly in a sauté pan.
2. With a fork, mix the dulse, lemon juice, and salt with the butter together until smooth.
3. Refrigerate until ready to use.

Variations, Ideas, Suggestions If your fishmonger doesn't have dulse or any other seaweed, and you happen to have some nori, toast and crumble an equivalent amount of that instead. If you happen to have a mortar and pestle available, grind the seaweed to a fine powder.

CHEESE FESTIVALS

Cheese is one of France's most beautiful gifts to the world of food, and there are festivals all over the country in spring and summer that celebrate this glorious expression of French expertise. Here are just a few. Consult the internet for more.

La Fête du Crottin de Chavignol: At the end of April in the Caves de la Mignonne at Sancerre you can enjoy tasting their marvelous goat cheese and all the festivities the town has to offer.

Les Fêtes des Fromages: The town of Pailherols, located in south-central France, celebrates the local Cantal cheese in early June with a cheese market. Local producers offer samples of this semi-hard cheese made from the Salers cows, which graze on the mountain meadows and pastures of the region.

Livarot Cheese Fair: The town of Livarot, set in the heart of Normandy's dairy region, hosts a festival that is devoted to cheese. The celebration includes a competition to find whoever can swallow the most at one sitting! The town is also home to a terrific cheese museum. What a great place for a cheesy weekend!

Chapter 5

BREAD AND PASTRY

(*Pain et Patisserie*)

"Good bread is the most
fundamentally satisfying of
all foods; and
good bread with fresh butter,
the greatest of feasts."

———

JAMES BEARD

Recipes featured in this chapter:

Pont-l'Évêque and Apple (Pomme) Tartine
Pear (Poire), Brie, and Thyme Tartine
Chèvre, Shallot (Echalote), Mushroom (Champignon),
and Bacon (Lardon) Tartine
Avocado (Avocat), Radish (Radis), and Seaweed Butter Tartine

I n France, no self-respecting man leaves the house without a scarf draped casually around his neck. In fact, almost every household we've visited has a rack near the front door with scarves of every description heaped on it. When we lived in Paris, every evening at precisely 6:55, Tim left our rented apartment without a word, wrapping his scarf around his neck as he shut the door. He hustled around the corner to catch the "last bake" of the day at the local boulangerie (bread shop). Fifteen minutes later he returned, beaming, gingerly holding the paper sleeve of a steaming hot baguette. The siren call of that irresistible aroma drifted up the stairwell before he opened the front door, bringing me close to drooling. Of course, he had honored another French custom when he chomped the pointed end of the loaf on his way home. Every evening on almost every street in the country, businessmen in suits and briefcases, women in stilettos and office attire, students in knee socks, and laborers in overalls stroll home carrying a fresh baguette with the top happily munched off. We'd sit down to dinner immediately so that our favorite unsalted butter from Normandy could melt into the crevices within the crusty bread's warm, soft interior. The baguette was so delicious that it made even my most ordinary culinary attempts seem delectable.

In the morning, Tim would repeat the process and dash out to the patisserie for hot, flaky croissants, or some other outrageous, addictive French concoction. This pattern went on whether we were in Paris, Lyon, or a tiny village. In the town of Semur-en-Auxois, located in Burgundy, our local boulangerie was owned by a large, red-faced, cheerful woman who perched on her stool near her cashbox. I never saw her move from her spot as she commanded her staff, mostly composed of her own brood, like a kindly Marine Corps drill instructor.

BREAD—THE HEART OF FRANCE

Baguette: That long, crusty loaf with the firm but meltingly delicious interior is what visitors dream of long after their time in France. The French consume ten billion baguettes annually, and they eat this satisfying bread at almost every meal. Even if you order a croque monsieur (a ham and cheese sandwich that's broiled or fried) or another bread dish in a restaurant, you'll probably be served a side of baguette slices, too.

For centuries, the baguette was a much larger loaf, but in the 1920s a law was passed in France that stated bakers couldn't work between 10 p.m. and 4 a.m., and so bakers began making the thin baguette we know today. That way they could start working at 4 a.m. and be ready for the morning rush.

Almost any time of day you'll see French people with a baguette tucked under their arm. There are even cunning little baguette carriers for the more fastidious. A baguette is usually about 25 inches long, and a demi-baguette is a sandwich-size length. And now, for those who forget to stop at the patisserie, there are vending machines all over France that will finish cooking the baguette and spit out a hot loaf on demand, 24-7!

Ficelle: This is the baguette's slimmer sister. It's sometimes topped with sesame seeds or cheese. It can be the same length or shorter than a regular baguette. They're great for making croutons, and when sliced they are a vehicle for getting dip from bowl to mouth.

Brioche: This light, puffy, semisweet bread is made with lots of butter and eggs. It can be made into many shapes, and it is considered a *viennoiserie* (dough made with yeast or puff pastry, often laminated) because it is made in the same basic way as bread, but with added liquid and other ingredients to make it more like a pastry. It's delicious on its own, but can also be used as a base for dessert toppings.

Fougasse: This bread resembles the Italian focaccia and is associated with Provence. It is usually shaped with slashes, so the loaf resembles a leaf or an ear of wheat. In Provence, olives, cheese, garlic, or anchovies are sometimes added. The French use this bread to make their mouth-watering version of the Italian calzone.

Pain de Campagne: Literally meaning "country bread," this round sourdough loaf is made with a combination of white and whole wheat flour or just whole wheat flour. It makes an amazing sandwich.

Pain Complet: This is another delicious loaf made with both whole wheat and white flour.

TARTINE—THE FRENCH SANDWICH

A word about the French tartine: This is one of France's most useful culinary inventions. The ingredients are always available, and you can be wildly creative. There is a baguette with your name on it in every village or city, and it's up to you to make yourself a brilliant meal.

Once, we endured the hottest summer recorded in Florence in more than a hundred years. We were so miserable, even with all the glorious art history and food to enjoy, that we fled to France where it was at least 25° cooler. We were in such a hurry to make our escape from that hot hell that Tim practically chose our next home in pin-the-tail-on-the-donkey fashion. His pin landed on a little village called La Charité-sur-Loire, a medieval town of 5,500 on the Loire river in the west of Burgundy, and we were lucky to book a *gîte* (vacation house) on the main street. We scurried through the mountains as fast as we could to reach that respite and spent two weeks reveling in pleasant weather and peaceful country living.

Our apartment was on the top floor of a medieval stone building, reached by a circular stone staircase with a sturdy rope handrail. Our grocery shopping was limited to what we could carry, so it was a good thing that the little town had a good selection of restaurants. The highlight of the spacious apartment was its tiny rooftop terrace, which was reached by a ladder. Once there, we could look directly down into the courtyard of the Abbey Church of Notre-Dame, an imposing twelfth-century church still in use today. It was a magical place for cocktails and nibbles as we watched the sun setting over those romantic medieval rooftops.

The country lanes along the river called to us almost every day, so we became expert tartine makers. The town's farmers' market was a perfect source for homemade cheese, bread, local fruit and vegetables, and fresh herbs, making it easy for us to put together delicious lunch spreads. We'd make our lunch in the morning, pack up some wine, hop aboard our rented bikes, and head out along the river into the country until we found a comfortable, shady spot to spread out our blanket. We'd spend the afternoon reading and enjoying the fresh air as we consumed our delicious treats. Those were among the most relaxing days we ever experienced during our five years on the road, and we still love making French-style lunches whenever we have the chance.

A NOTE ABOUT BREAKFAST FOR KIDS

If you are traveling with school-age children, there is much for them to enjoy, like chocolate croissants (*pain au chocolat*), baguette with butter and preserves, hot chocolate, apple pastry (*chausson aux pomme*), plus juice. Breakfast is ridiculously easy to prepare in France, and we're betting they won't miss their Froot Loops one bit. Of course, you can certainly do as the French do and have yogurt and fruit for breakfast!

PASTRY (*Patisserie*)

We could spend pages and pages describing the astonishing varieties of pastry that will tempt you a hundred times a day as you wander through France, but that would be a ridiculous waste of your time. Writing recipes for these decadent delights would be even sillier, since you will be surrounded by excellent bakeries, and trying to bake in a sparingly equipped vacation kitchen would be a real trial.

We know you'll choose all by yourself, because your own eyes will tell you which pastries are most appealing. We'll list a few of the most popular pastries, but do trust your own instincts. We know you'll enjoy every luxurious morsel.

Baba au Rhum: A small yeast cake which is saturated in a hard liquor syrup. It's sometimes filled with whipped cream or pastry cream.

Canelé: This delightful pastry from Bordeaux is creamy on the inside and crispy and caramelized on the outside. It has a heady rum and vanilla aroma, and is not to be missed when visiting the area.

Clafoutis aux Cerises: The classic is made with cherries, but almost any fruit will be divine when a thick, creamy batter is poured over it. The batter puffs up over the fruit and becomes almost like a tender cake.

Éclair: This famous delight comes in chocolate, vanilla, coffee, pistachio, and other amazing flavors.

Kouign Amann: This pastry hails from Brittany and is made from a dough similar to a croissant, but is round with a caramelized sugar crust.

Macaron: This colorful French sandwich cookie has taken the world by storm. They are made with egg whites, creating a meringue, and are usually filled with either jam or ganache.

Mille-Feuille: Very thin layers of pastry and pastry cream make up this ethereal pastry.

Mousse au Chocolat: Chocolate mousse—a fluffy, smooth confection of cream and chocolate.

Tarte Tatin: This treat is almost like an upside-down apple tart. The apples are caramelized before being put into the pastry.

Tarts: You will find different types of tarts of all sizes. Many feature a cream filling and are topped with fresh fruit and gorgeous glazes.

TARTINE

THROUGHOUT RECORDED HISTORY, man has combined flour and water and then cooked it, piled other edibles on it, and consumed it. However, none of these many configurations can compare with the French tartine—a crusty baguette with its soft pillowy interior slathered with cheese, mayonnaise, oil, or butter, and topped off with an endless choice of sweet and savory ingredients. We've included some ideas to get you started!

Pont-l'Évêque and Apple (*Pomme*) Tartine

—— SERVES 4 ——

This cheese's rich, creamy flavor and supple consistency are the perfect qualities to balance the sweet crunchiness of the apples. It's sure to be a hit any time of day.

INGREDIENTS

4 ounces (120 g) Pont-l'Évêque cheese, cold and sliced
4 slices of white or brown bread, toasted
4 tablespoons (60 ml) salted butter
2 apples, cored and sliced
Salt
1 tablespoon (15 g) minced thyme

EQUIPMENT

Knife for slicing
Medium sauté pan

Method

1. Place the cheese slices evenly on the toasts.
2. Melt the butter in a sauté pan on medium-high heat. When bubbling, add the apple slices. Sauté until golden brown. Sprinkle with salt. Spoon over the toasts.
3. Sprinkle with thyme and serve.

Variations, Ideas, Suggestions

- Try adding a spoonful of brown sugar to the apple slices when sautéing.
- You don't have to use Pont-l'Évêque. Other soft cheeses will also be wonderful.

Pear (*Poire*), Brie, and Thyme Tartine

—— SERVES 4 ——

These ingredients were made for each other—the nutty Brie and pear are a perfect pair, and the thyme adds snap to both of them.

INGREDIENTS

1 baguette
Butter
Salt
1 pear, cored and thinly sliced
4 ounces (112 g) Brie, or another
    cheese that will melt nicely,
    thinly sliced
2 teaspoons (10 g) chopped thyme
1 ounce (30 g) honey

EQUIPMENT

Knife for slicing

Method

1. Slice baguette in half lengthwise, then crosswise.
2. Broil until lightly toasted, 1 to 2 minutes. Spread lightly with butter and sprinkle with salt.
3. Top with pear slices, then cheese.
4. Broil until cheese is melted, about 2 to 3 minutes.
5. Sprinkle with thyme and drizzle with a little bit of honey.

Chèvre, Shallot (*Échalote*), Mushroom (*Champignon*), and Bacon (*Lardon*) Tartine

———— SERVES 4 ————

This recipe takes the sandwich to new heights. That subtle garlic flavor of the shallot enhances the earthy mushroom and salty bacon. Make a big batch because they will go fast!

INGREDIENTS

¼ to ½ pound (113–225 g) *lardons* (or diced bacon)
1 pound (450 g) mushrooms, wiped clean and roughly chopped into about ½-inch (13 mm) pieces
1 cup (100 g) shallots, cut into about ½-inch (13 mm) pieces
3 tablespoons (45 ml) olive oil, if needed
Salt
Pepper
4 thick slices of white chewy, crusty bread
4 ounces (120 g) chèvre
1 tablespoon (15 g) minced thyme or parsley

EQUIPMENT

Baking sheet
Knife
Measuring cups and spoons
Medium sauté pan
Slotted spoon or spatula

Method

1. Preheat the oven to 450°F (230°C).
2. In a medium sauté pan, add the *lardons* and turn on the heat to medium. Let cook slowly, turning down the heat if necessary, until the *lardons* are rendered and golden brown. Fish out the *lardons* with a slotted spoon or spatula and set aside. Pour off all but a cou-

Continued

ple of tablespoons (30 ml) of the fat into a heatproof dish of some kind. Do not discard.

3. On a baking sheet, toss the mushrooms, shallots, 3 tablespoons *lardon* fat (if there's not enough, add some olive oil), salt, and pepper until very lightly coated. Make sure they are in one layer so that the steam from cooking can escape. If the steam can't escape, then the mushroom and shallots will be mushy and will not caramelize. If necessary, use two pans.

4. Bake for about 20 minutes. If not yet golden, cook longer.

5. While the mushroom mixture is baking, turn the stovetop heat back on to medium and when the *lardon* fat left in the pan is lightly sizzling, sauté the bread on both sides until golden. Set aside.

6. Right before the mushroom mixture is finished, spread the chèvre on the toasts. Mix the *lardons* into the mushroom mixture and spoon over the toasts.

7. Sprinkle with thyme, adjust seasoning, and serve.

Variations, Ideas, Suggestions

- This dish is also nice when topped with a few leaves of chervil, or chervil lightly dressed as a side salad, or with a poached egg on top.
- If using bacon, feel free to cook the whole slices and dice after cooking.
- Made too much? Breakfast the next day! Add a poached egg on some warmed mushroom mixture. Or for dinner, blend the mixture with some pasta and cream.
- Wait to adjust seasoning until after you've added the *lardons* or bacon, as they add a lot of salt to the dish.

Avocado (*Avocat*), Radish (*Radis*), and Seaweed Butter Tartine

—— SERVES 4 ——

Your guests will be amazed by this colorful invention. The spicy radish flavor is a great foil for the creamy avocado and exotic seaweed butter.

INGREDIENTS

Sea salt
2 ripe avocados, halved with pits removed
3 tablespoons (45 ml) olive oil
4 thick slices of chewy, crusty white bread
1 tablespoon (15 ml) butter
2 very fresh radishes, very thinly sliced
4 tablespoons (60 ml) Seaweed Butter (see page 95)

EQUIPMENT

Fork for mashing
Knife for slicing and cutting
Medium sauté pan

Method

1. Sprinkle a little salt on each avocado half. Mash, while still in its skin, with a fork.

2. Heat the olive oil in a sauté pan on medium heat. Brown the bread slices in the pan on each side until lightly golden. Remove from pan.

3. With the heat still on, melt the butter in the sauté pan and toss in the very thinly sliced radishes. Sauté for about one minute, toss in a little sea salt to taste, and remove from pan. The goal is for them to still be crisp. They should be just warmed and buttery.

4. Slather each bread slice on one side with the seaweed butter, then scoop out the mashed avocado and pile on each slice. Sprinkle with sea salt, top with the radish slices, and devour.

Variations, Ideas, Suggestions   If you happen to have a mandoline and can get the radish slices extremely thin so that they are transparent, then you don't really need to sauté them. If you have a mandoline, but are not used to using one, then be careful with your fingers.

Chapter 6

POULTRY

(Volaille)

"The best way to
execute French cooking
is to get good and loaded
and whack the hell
out of a chicken. *Bon appétit*!"

———

JULIA CHILD

Recipes featured in this chapter:

*Pan-Roasted Duck Breast (*Magret de Canard)
with Seared Mirabelle Plums
*Chicken (*Poulet) *with Tomatoes and Olives*
*Guinea Fowl (*Pintade) *à la Normande*
*Rabbit (*Lapin) *with Prunes (*Pruneaux)
Pearl Couscous

P eople who have a chance to live, even for a little while, in La Belle France get to experience her culinary blessings, such as living cheese that hasn't been killed with pasteurizing heat, chicken that tastes like the real thing, and some of the most heavenly wines in the world. One of her unique gifts is the availability of what I firmly believe is God's poultry gift to man: duck. Duck is to the French as chicken is to Americans. We'll get to the part about eating the duck itself later in this chapter, but first I want to extol the virtues of its stunning by-product, duck fat. If you have not cooked with this indispensable ingredient, you're in for an astounding revelation. Its smoking point is higher than butter, and it's fabulous for frying and flavoring potatoes, mushrooms, greens, popcorn, and almost anything else. It also has less saturated fats than butter or bacon! In any French market, you'll see many kinds of duck fat crowding the butter case, but in the United States, it's not so readily available. I've resorted to ordering jars of it online. It keeps in the refrigerator for ages, although it doesn't last long enough at our house for me to tell you exactly how long. It's expensive, but because its flavor is so distinct and it's good for you relative to similar fats, it's worth the splurge. You can find it on Amazon and many specialty grocery websites. Now that I've done my bit to make your cooking experience better with this divine, silky, yellow miracle, we'll talk about the bird itself.

DUCK (*Canard*)

One warm summer day, as Tim and I strolled along Rue Vaugirard near our first apartment in Paris, he stopped abruptly, annoying the small French lady who was bustling along close to his heels. When I looked at him in alarm he pointed to the little store next to us. It was a shop devoted entirely to duck!

There were towers of tinned duck, jarred duck, duck pâté, cassoulet, and many other goodies that I couldn't identify. There were frozen ducks and duck parts in the freezer case, fresh duck, and even pre-prepared duck confit in the cool cases. There were books about duck, posters of ducks lolling around ponds and swimming in rivers, and anatomical drawings of duck parts.

"Only in France," I thought.

A little bell on the door tinkled as we entered, and through a bright yellow curtain at the back of the store came Madame Allard, who was destined to become a great pal and instructor about all things duck-related.

After our bonjours she switched to English. She was amused at our enthusiasm and our surprise at finding a store dedicated solely to our favorite fowl, and we spent half an hour admiring her stock while that little bell rang with other customers' arrivals. Of course, our little plaid cart was brimming with pâté, duck breast, duck fat, and a cute little recipe book in English.

That very night I made my first attempt at cooking a duck breast. I had phoned Deborah first to confirm what the little book had told me. I was very proud of myself when Tim congratulated me on a great meal, and I was able to add another dish to my repertoire.

If I can do it, so can you! If you're ever going to cook duck, now is the time to try it. When you go to the market, or better yet the *boucherie* in France, you'll find it easily.

CHICKEN (*Poulet*)

When we travel to France, and many other countries for that matter, I am always surprised the first time I order chicken in a restaurant or cook it in our rental kitchen. The raw chickens in the markets almost always have a yellow tinge to their skin, which can be a little alarming until you realize that those free-range birds have been pecking away at marigold seeds or sometimes corn. Since they aren't pumped up with water and hormones, they're smaller than what we typically get in the United States. And here's the very best part: These birds taste like chicken! Those of us of a certain age can remember what chicken tasted like years ago, back when we were children. So if you're one of us, you're in for a little tastebud déjà vu in France when you eat chicken.

To further your trip back in time, there might even be a couple of pinfeathers left on the bird. Just make sure to remove them before cooking. In Ireland, where I lived for a few years in the early '90s, the chickens came with more than a few pinfeathers, too many to pluck by hand. My neighbor taught me to zap the fowl over an open flame to make the feathers disappear. It smelled awful but certainly did the job. The French are more fastidious about feathers, so searing the bird won't be necessary.

A proper French butcher would never dream of expecting you to deal with pinfeathers, globs of fat, sinew, or anything you wouldn't want to eat. It will cost you a few more bucks to shop with the butcher than at a grocery story, but it will be infinitely more fun and you'll get better-quality poultry in the bargain.

GUINEA FOWL (*Pintade*)

Guinea fowl or guinea hens are uncommon in the United States, where they are quite expensive and not easy to find. The French consume them with gusto, because these relatives of chickens, pheasants, and partridges have roughly half the fat of chicken and marginally more protein than turkey. Their meat is dark and reminiscent of pheasant, but less gamey. Their eggs are substantially richer than chicken eggs.

RABBIT (*Lapin*)

You may wonder about finding a rabbit recipe tucked into the poultry section of this book, but the fact is that rabbit is a common and delicious source of protein and is served in many cultures. France, Italy, and Spain produce and consume more rabbit than any other countries in Europe. In Italy, it's usually doused in some flavorful concoction and braised to ensure a tender and moist result; the French by contrast favor mustard as their classic flavor. Rabbit is enjoying a wave of popularity in the United States, where the public is learning to separate what's on their plate from their memory of Brer Rabbit or that sweet little bunny their third-grade class raised. Let's face it, many of us eat cute little lambs, fluffy chicks, and relatives of Bambi without a thought, so why not rabbit? Rabbit meat is all-white meat, low in fat, high in protein, and relatively low in cholesterol and sodium. What's more, it's highly palatable and easily digested. Rabbit has a higher percentage of protein and a lower percentage of fat than chicken, turkey, beef, or pork. Not only is it a source rich in unsaturated omega fatty acids, but it is also a lean source of protein that can be substituted for red meat and poultry in most recipes. So set aside your squeamishness, get out that ovenproof pot, and start a new cooking adventure!

DUCK (*Canard*)

IF YOU HAVE BEEN reluctant to attempt cooking duck, this recipe will change your mind. Just follow Deborah's recipe and you will feel like a duck expert.

Pan-Roasted Duck Breast (*Magret de Canard*) with Seared Mirabelle Plums

—— SERVES 4 ——

Deborah's cousin grows stone fruit in California's Central Valley. They have so much of it that she was inspired to devise ways to put it on her restaurant's menu. This recipe, which was a big hit with customers, was inspired by her friend Chris Wright, owner of the intimate Parisian restaurant Le Timbre on Rue Sainte-Beuve in the 6th arrondissement. The two chefs, who met sitting at a bar in the Pigalle neighborhood of Paris, opened their restaurants within months of each other and have remained great friends. Chris is masterful at combining fresh, simple tastes, as you'll see when you try this easy, flavorful duck breast.

INGREDIENTS

4 duck breasts, skin on
Salt
Pepper
Other spices (alone or a mixture),
    such as coriander, ground fennel,
    ground ginger, tiny bit of ground
    clove (optional)
5 mirabelle plums, or other
    plums, firm but ripe, quartered
    (or peaches)
2 tablespoons (30 ml) brandy
2 tablespoons (30 ml) honey
Juice from ½ orange
¼ teaspoon (.5 g) orange zest
1 teaspoon (5 g) chopped fresh
    thyme

EQUIPMENT

Knife for slicing and chopping
Large sauté pan
Measuring spoons

Continued

Method

1. Trim excess fat off the breasts and score the skin by quickly drawing your sharpened knife across the skin diagonally six or seven times, then do it again in the opposite direction so that a diamond pattern is created.

2. Season with salt and pepper plus other spices, if you wish.

3. In a cold sauté pan, sprinkle about ¼ teaspoon (1.5 g) of salt, and place breasts skin side down, leaving room between each breast. Turn the heat on low and let cook until the skin becomes golden brown. Keep the temperature low. This will render the fat and create a crispy skin. Depending on the thickness of the breast, this could take between 10 and 15 minutes. The breast should be almost finished.

4. Turn the breast over and finish cooking for about 5 more minutes. Be careful not to overcook.

5. Pull the breasts out of the pan and let them rest no more than 10 minutes.

6. Immediately, while the duck is resting, pour all but about 1 tablespoon of the duck fat out of the pan (and reserve it for another use!). Turn up the heat to the highest setting. When it's hot, toss in the plum quarters and sear quickly, turning them over after about 30 seconds. You don't want them to get mushy.

7. Deglaze with the brandy. Add the honey, orange juice, and orange zest. Season with salt and pepper.

8. Cut each breast, diagonally, into 3 pieces. Put either on dinner plates or on a platter if you are serving family style. Put the plums on the plates or the platter. Drizzle the sauce over the duck and sprinkle with thyme.

Pairing   Red Bordeaux or Pinot Noir

CHICKEN (*Poulet*)

LIKE ALMOST EVERYTHING ELSE, the French have a way with chicken—or should I say many ways?

Chicken (*Poulet*) with Tomatoes and Olives

—— SERVES 4 ——

This dish, which can be easily re-created almost anywhere on earth, is satisfying soul food. Just the ticket when you're tired and want a simple meal in a hurry.

INGREDIENTS

21 garlic cloves
4 tablespoons (60 ml) olive oil, divided, plus more for drizzling
1½ teaspoons (12 g) *piment d'espelette* or red pepper flakes (if not available, use half black pepper and half paprika)
2 teaspoons (10 ml) soy sauce or tamari
1 large chicken, pinfeathers removed, quartered
Sea salt
2 pounds (900 g) fresh tomatoes, whatever kind you like; halved or quartered if large, or you can use whole grape tomatoes

2 small heads escarole, cut into 6 wedges each
½ cup (125 ml) Castelvetrano or picholine olives, pitted (or olive of your choice)
2 tablespoons (30 ml) olive juice
3 sprigs thyme, finely chopped, plus more for garnish
1 crusty baguette, sliced in half lengthwise

EQUIPMENT

Knife for chopping and slicing
Measuring cups and spoons
Large baking dish
Large spoon

Method

1. Preheat oven to 450°F (235°C). Finely chop one garlic clove and mix it with 1 tablespoon (15 ml) of the olive oil, pepper, and soy sauce. Rub this all over the chicken pieces, then season with salt.

2. In a large baking dish, toss tomatoes, escarole, the remaining garlic cloves, olives, olive juice, and thyme with the remaining 3 tablespoons (45 ml) of olive oil. Season with salt and black pepper.

3. Arrange chicken on top of the tomato mixture.

4. Roast until brown and cooked through, 45 to 50 minutes.

5. Remove chicken from the pan to rest.

6. Put the vegetables back in the oven.

7. Drizzle olive oil on open side of the baguette halves, season with salt, and stick on the top shelf in the oven for about five minutes or until nicely toasted. Cut each piece of baguette in half to make four servings.

8. Put the lightly toasted baguette pieces in 4 large soup/pasta bowls or on dinner plates.

9. Place a quarter chicken in each bowl on the bread, and spoon the vegetables around the chicken. Spoon over the pan juices and sprinkle with more fresh thyme.

Pairing Red Bordeaux

Variations, Ideas, Suggestions

- You could substitute summer squash for the escarole if that suits your taste.
- For a vegetarian version, substitute small halved potatoes, roasting onions, or summer squash for the chicken. Add some white wine to the roasting liquid. Top the toasted bread with the vegetable mixture, then some mozzarella, and put back in the oven to slightly melt the cheese. Top with fresh thyme.

TIP: *To peel garlic cloves more easily, start by rolling them gently under the flat side of a large knife blade first.*

GUINEA FOWL (*Pintade*)

I REMEMBER hearing the phrase "Guinea hen under glass" when I was a child. It meant that something elegant, exotic, and expensive was about to be presented at the table. In France, it's an everyday menu item—certainly not served under a glass dome!

Guinea Fowl (*Pintade*) à la Normande

—— SERVES 4 ——

If you're in France, you really should take the opportunity to try this luscious recipe.

INGREDIENTS

4 airline guinea fowl breast halves, skin on (a full airline is chef-speak for the partial wing bone still attached to the breast for added flavor and presentation)
Salt
Pepper
4 tablespoons (60 ml) butter or olive oil
4 apples, cut into 1 to 2-inch (25–50 mm) pieces
2 turnips, cut into 1 to 2-inch (25–50mm) pieces
¼ cup (60 ml) brandy
¼ cup (60 ml) cream
½ cup (120 ml) chicken stock or broth
½ cup (120 ml) apple juice
2 tablespoons (30 g) chopped thyme

EQUIPMENT

Knife for chopping and slicing
Large ovenproof pan
Measuring cups and spoons
Tongs or a fork for turning meat

Method

1. Preheat oven to 350°F (180°C).
2. Season the guinea fowl with salt and pepper.
3. Heat butter in an ovenproof pan on medium-high heat. Add the fowl and brown evenly on all sides.
4. Add apple and turnips and sauté until golden brown. If there is no room in the pan for the apple and turnip, then remove the fowl first. When the apple and turnips are golden, add the fowl back and deglaze with brandy.
5. Add cream, stock, and apple juice, cover the pan and put in oven for about 30 minutes. If you don't have an oven, just lower the flame and cook for about 30 minutes, covered. Check the turnips and breasts for doneness. Adjust seasonings.
6. Slice the guinea fowl breasts and serve with sauce spooned over the top and apples and turnips on the side. Sprinkle thyme over the fowl.

Pairing Grenache, Pinot Noir, Rhône white, Côte de Beaune

RABBIT (*Lapin*)

DEBORAH HAS DEVELOPED a different take on the traditional French rabbit dish. She's added some capers, which makes it somewhat reminiscent of the *Silver Palate Cookbook* classic Chicken Marbella dish. If you can't bring yourself to experiment with rabbit, this recipe is just as mouthwatering if you substitute chicken.

Rabbit (*Lapin*) with Prunes (*Pruneaux*)

—— SERVES 4 ——

Use one rabbit, cut into pieces, as you would a chicken—
about 2 ½ pounds (1.25 kg). If the rabbit is very small,
you may need two. Weigh the pieces, not the whole rabbit.
(We recommend having the butcher cut the rabbit.)

INGREDIENTS

16 prunes, pitted
¼ cup (60 ml) brandy
Approximately 2½ pounds
    (1.25 kg) rabbit pieces
Salt
Pepper
Flour for dusting (optional)
3 tablespoons (45 ml) vegetable oil
6 cloves garlic, finely minced
¼ cup (60 ml) plus 3 tablespoons
    (45 ml) olive oil
1½ cups (350 ml) white wine (you
    can substitute red wine if that's
    what you have on hand)
1 cup (250 ml) chicken stock
¼ cup (60 ml) red wine vinegar or
    another similar vinegar
2 tablespoons (30 ml) Dijon
    mustard (smooth)
2 tablespoons (30 g) capers
2 tablespoons (30 ml) caper liquid
    from the jar of capers
¼ cup (50 g) brown sugar
3 sprigs fresh thyme
Chopped parsley
Pearl Couscous (page 135), for serving

EQUIPMENT

Bowl
Measuring cups and spoons
Medium ovenproof pot with cover

Method

1. Preheat the oven to 300°F (150°C).
2. Place the prunes in a bowl and pour the brandy over. Set aside and let soak.
3. Season the rabbit pieces with salt and pepper. Then dust with flour, if using.
4. Heat the vegetable oil in ovenproof pot on medium-high heat and lightly brown the rabbit pieces in batches. Remove rabbit and set aside.
5. Lower the heat and let the pan cool down a bit, then add the garlic and 3 tablespoons of olive oil, and simmer until fragrant, about 2 minutes—do not brown the garlic or it will be bitter. Deglaze with the wine, scraping the sides of the pan to release the fond (tasty bits).
6. Add the rabbit, chicken stock, vinegar, mustard, ¼ cup olive oil, capers, caper liquid, brown sugar, thyme, and prunes with brandy.
7. Cover and bake in the oven for about 1 hour, stirring occasionally.
8. Remove the lid and cook for another half hour, until the rabbit (or chicken) is very tender. Remove the thyme sprigs.
9. Serve in bowls or plates on top of Pearl Couscous (see page 135), with plenty of the braising liquid spooned over.
10. Sprinkle with chopped parsley, or you can serve with the Roasted Carrots in the Entertaining chapter (see page 47) and top with minced carrot tops.

Pairing   Côtes de Bourg, Alsacian Pinot Gris, mead

Continued

Variations, Ideas, Suggestions

- If the sauce is not thick enough for you, after removing the rabbit and the prunes, reduce a bit more and then spoon it over the rabbit.
- If you don't have an oven, or it's unreliable, you can simmer on the stove, covered, for about 1½ hours until tender.
- Try leaving the brown sugar out of the braising liquid, sprinkle it on the rabbit, and bake uncovered at 350°F (180°C) for about 50 minutes or until the meat is separating from the bone. This will naturally reduce the liquid and crisp up the rabbit a bit.
- Also great with polenta or potato purée, if you're so inclined to make it. Or try it with a delicious white bean ragout.
- You could leave the capers out of the dish and fry them in a pan with about a half inch of oil until crispy, and then sprinkle them over the plated dish. But don't omit the caper liquid.

Pearl Couscous

Pearl couscous, also called Israeli couscous, is larger in size than traditional couscous. Try lightly toasting the couscous until barely golden on a sheet pan in a 350°F (180°C) oven. This will add an interesting toasty flavor. You can also toast the couscous in a large sauté pan on medium heat. Make sure to keep shaking the pan so the pearls toast evenly.

INGREDIENTS

⅔ cups (150 ml) chicken broth
⅔ cup (150 ml) water
1 cup (150 g) pearl couscous
¼ teaspoon (1.5 g) cinnamon
¼ teaspoon (1.5 g) sea salt

EQUIPMENT

Medium saucepan with a snug-
  fitting lid
Measuring cups and spoons

Method

1. Add the stock and water to a medium saucepan and bring to a boil.
2. Add the couscous, cinnamon, and salt. Reduce the heat and simmer, tightly covered, until water is absorbed, about 10 minutes.
3. Remove from the heat and let stand, still covered, for about 3 more minutes.
4. Remove the lid and fluff a bit with a fork. Serve.

Variations, Ideas, Suggestions

- Cook with vegetable stock or salted water if you would like to serve the couscous with something vegetarian.
- Toss with Roasted Cauliflower (*Chou-Fleur*) with Currants and Capers (see page 209) and some sautéed kale for a lovely warm salad for lunch or dinner.

Chapter 7

MEAT

(Viande)

"If it has four legs
and it's not a table,
eat it."

———

CANTONESE SAYING

Recipes featured in this chapter:

*Hanger Steak (*Onglet*) with Sautéed Mushrooms
(*Cépes*), Cream, and Brandy*
*Beef (*Boeuf*) Bourguignon*
*Pork Loin (*Longe de Porc*) with Apples (*Pommes*) and Onions*
*Mead and Honey Braised Lamb Shanks (*Souris d'Agneau*)*
*Lentils (*Lentilles*) with Andouille and Vinaigrette*

In France, cattle and other animals destined for French dining rooms are not fed or injected with hormones or other additives. They are primarily free range, which makes their meat healthier for the consumer and better for the environment. When livestock are grass fed, topsoils aren't depleted by raising feed, and the pigs, sheep, and cattle themselves provide the fertilizer. The French eat about 39 percent less meat (this means beef, pork, and sheep) per capita than people in the United States. This statistic may contribute to the annoying fact that the French also claim a much lower rate of obesity. When I stroll down almost any busy street in France, it's fairly easy to tell who the locals are—not just because the tourists have cameras slung around their necks and are sporting shorts and flip-flops, but because their girth is noticeably wider. And let us not forget that the French usually have better haircuts!

You can buy acceptable meat in most of the supermarkets, where you can grab a wrapped package from the meat case without having to stress over interacting with a live person—in French, no less. But if you plan your menu so that you have a good sense of what you're after, and maybe have a slug of wine to buoy up your courage, you, too, can manage to buy meat or poultry at a specialty shop. The effort is worth the trouble, because what you'll get is superior to what's available at Carrefour or Intermarché. Don't be intimidated about asking *un boucher* to help. In France, even if the butcher doesn't speak English, it's almost a sure bet that someone waiting in line can. And although French people can look dour when shopping, they are generally very kind and willing to help. I mean, who's joyfully grinning while waiting in a line anywhere? If you're lucky enough to stay in a particular neighborhood for a while, you may get to know your *boucher* well. Don't forget your local farmers' market, which can be an excellent source for your meat and poultry needs. Let's dive in and learn about buying and cooking meat the French way.

BEEF (*Boeuf*)

The two most popular cattle breeds are the Limousin, which are a bright reddish-brown color, and the white Charolais. Both animals have inward-curving horns and are considered to be the highest quality. In French markets, the breed will be on the label as well as the words *race à viande*, that is, cattle raised for beef. You might also see other breeds like Amoricaine, Aubrac, or Lourdais in the market.

Although those big beautiful animals that lounge in tall grass under luminous French skies may look like the ones that provide beef elsewhere, North Americans are sometimes surprised to find that French beef does not taste quite the same as what they find at home. Because French livestock are not fed or injected with hormones or other additives, and are primarily free range, their meat is less fatty. The lower fat content means French beef isn't always as tasty as the grain-fed beef found in the United States. You'll just need to make some adjustments in order to produce food that will taste as good as the cows look.

Keep in mind that because of the limited fat marbling in French beef, overcooking will ruin the meat and make it extremely tough. If you like your beef on the done side, without much pink showing, then choose a cut for braising. Long and slow cooking in liquid will render the meat tender and tasty.

The French, like most people in the world, use all parts of the animal in some way. In the market or meat shop, you'll find brains, kidneys, liver, heart, and lung right alongside the steaks and roasts. One of our favorite restaurants in Paris, Chez L'Ami Jean, has a months-long waiting list for clientele who are willing to endure the crowd to savor its famous beef sausage and delicious dishes using the tongue, sweetbreads, and even the tail of animals. This famous restaurant is crowded, loud, and the service brusque, but the steaming platters of deeply flavorful meat that the waiters manage to wrangle over the heads of patrons bring such exquisite pleasure that people don't care.

We became such fans of offal (organ meats) that we'd regularly travel across Paris to a tiny restaurant called Le Baratin, where chefs from around the city came to eat a superb, cheap lunch and share the latest restaurant gossip. We learned to love kidneys, beef cheeks, and one of my favorites, liver, which were perfectly prepared and served in a convivial atmosphere.

Here's a vital cooking tip, whether you're cooking on the road or in your own kitchen at home: Don't be afraid to try to cook something new. After all, it's just *food*, not an international peace treaty. If you mess it up, the worst that can happen is that you get taken out to dinner instead and the dog next door gets a yummy feast! To give yourself a leg up on your challenge, ask the butcher to tell you how the meat you are buying should be handled. That way you're less likely to end up producing shoe leather instead of the savory dish you had in mind.

So let's pretend you've bought just the right piece of meat—a steak—brought it home, and unwrapped it in your cute little kitchen. First, mix about a teaspoon of salt and any other spices you are using, like pepper, cumin, oregano, or paprika, or all of them, with some crushed garlic. Rub it all over the meat and let it sit on the counter for an hour or two. This will allow the seasoning to penetrate the meat, and it will also bring the meat up to room temperature so it will cook more evenly.

Before cooking, wipe off the salt and spices and pat the meat dry. Make your pan as hot as you can and sear the steak on both sides. Then lower the heat to cook to either medium rare or rare. If you're not sure, make a small incision to check or use a handy instant thermometer. Rare should be at 130°F (54°C) and medium rare at 140°F (60°C). Grass-fed beef cooks fast, so be watchful after the sear. Season it again and, to make up for the lack of fat, drizzle a little olive oil or melted butter over your steak, and then serve it with *savoir-faire*. The same rules apply for roasting meat. Cook a roast at about 225°F (107°C) to 250°F (121°C). A general rule of thumb is to cook all French beef 30 percent less than you would cook American beef.

A solemn warning about French steak: Even though you will be very tempted to marinate your French steak, don't do it. Adding a lot of moisture will make it difficult to brown, and you may end up with an unappetizing steamed mess.

Cuts of Beef (*Bouef*)

Our favorite steak cuts are:

Entrecôte (ribeye)—
flavorful and juicy

Onglet (hanger steak)—
resembles flank steak

Faux filet (sirloin)—a little
tougher but more flavorful

Filet (filet mignon)—
tender, juicy, expensive

Pavé or *filet de romsteck*—similar
but not as tender as filet
mignon

Bavette d'aloyau—similar to
flank steak but more tender

For stews or braises try:

Paleron and *macreuse* and
jumeau—all similar to chuck

Gros bout de poitrine—a brisket

Gite—round steak

PORK (*Porc*)

The French are prodigious pork producers, consumers, and export-
ers. While the majority of the swine are grown on the west coast
around Brittany, boutique farmers, like the ones from Limousin, who
practice sustainable growth and keep traditional methods to raise their
free-range pigs, produce superior meat. In that area, many farms breed
black-bottomed pigs (*cul noir*), which have color patterns that look
somewhat like Yves Saint Laurent's geometrical designs in black and
beige. These haute porkers can turn a simple pork chop dinner into a
memorable culinary treat.

Once again, like most countries in the world, the French eat almost the entire animal, nose to tail. The ears, feet, and head might be considered the nasty bits here at home, but in France those parts are delicacies. We hope that you'll have the fortitude to try them when you have the opportunity.

If you are a fan of pork tenderloin, look for *filet de mignon de porc.* If bacon is on your menu, be aware that bacon in France is more like the lean Canadian bacon than the crispy strips you'll get in the United States. The best substitute for American bacon is *poitrine,* which is a cut from the breast of the pig. But don't expect to find an Oscar Mayer or Hormel pound of bacon. Instead, be on the lookout for a diced bacon product called *lardons.* These brilliant bits of flavor, which come in *nature* (plain) or *fumé* (smoked) forms, are mostly pork fat that's been cut into small pieces. They are good in quiches and any other dish calling for crumbled bacon. Once you've had them in your refrigerator, you won't know how you lived without them. For instance, if you're staring at a pile of boring green beans trying to figure out something to do with them, pop a handful of *lardons* into a pan, render their fat, and bang in the beans. The flavor and the crunch will make you happy! Of course, if you're feeling extra peppy, you could throw in some garlic and maybe some fresh herbs to up your game.

Cuts of Pork (*Porc*)

Poitrine (bacon)—ask for it to be sliced fine (pronounced *feen*) or it will be cut thicker than you are used to

Ventrèche (French pancetta)

Lardons (fatty bacon)

Echine (shoulder)

Côtes de porc (a rack of loin chops)

Longe de porc (pork loin)

Filet de mignon de porc (pork tenderloin)

LAMB (*Agneau*)

belong to a long line of dedicated lambophiles. Family celebrations like birthdays, Easter, even Christmas, usually mean the designated hostess is going to be intimately acquainted with one or more lamb legs, depending on the number of celebrants who will belly up to the table. We do succumb to tradition and wrangle a turkey to the table for

Thanksgiving, but otherwise, we are devoted to ovine feasts. The most exquisite-tasting lamb I've ever had was served at Château d'Agneaux, a thirteenth-century château in Northern France. As attractive and historic as the château itself was, my lamb dinner in the hotel's restaurant was the highlight of the weekend. The meat, cooked simply, was perfectly pink and moist and had a distinct flavor that I couldn't quite identify. Later, I was telling Deborah about our weekend trip, describing the hotel, the lovely countryside, and the sites we had enjoyed. I asked her if she knew why the lamb flavor was so unusual. Of course, my brilliant friend had the answer: Since the lambs graze near the sea, the grass they eat is bathed in a salty brine. You could say that their meat is salted from the inside out!

Cuts of Lamb (*Agneau*)

Gigot d'agneau (leg of lamb)

Souris d'agneau or *jarret* (shank)

Echine (shoulder)

Carré d'agneau (rack of lamb)

Côtelette (lamb rack chop)

SAUSAGE—DRY OR COOKED
(*Saucisse; Saucisson*)

Sampling and cooking with some of the great sausages the French produce is one of the joys of eating like a local in France. The variety of sausage is astounding, and every region has its specialties. Not only are there the kinds we would expect to see, but there are fish sausages and even vegetarian sausages. Many classic French meals include sausage, like cassoulet and lentils, and it is also a significant feature of picnic baskets and hors d'oeuvre spreads. Sausages of all kinds are available everywhere, and it's helpful to be acquainted with some of the more popular ones so that you can feel a little more confident in your sausage choices.

Generally speaking, unless the sign says otherwise, you can safely assume that the sausage you're buying in a charcuterie (deli) is made with pork. The others will be labeled to show what meat, fish, or other ingredients are in the sausage.

Andouille is made with pig intestines and many other ingredients. It is usually precooked.

Boudin Blanc is thought of as white blood sausage, but it's actually made from white pork, chicken, or veal meat with some seasoning. They are often precooked and are great when reheated and served with mashed potatoes.

Boudin Noir is made with pork blood and other ingredients like raisins, chestnuts, apples, or prunes. Buy this very fresh and cook it thoroughly in a pan or grilled.

Cervelas is very popular in Alsace and originated in Switzerland. This sausage is fat and juicy, and it fans out because its ends are sliced. It is sold both cooked and uncooked.

Chipolata is made from pork with herb seasonings. It is also a favorite at French barbecues.

Figatellu is a Corsican specialty. Made from pork liver and tons of garlic, it is great grilled or in a sauce.

Merguez is usually made from lamb, but sometimes beef is included. It is dark red because of the spices mixed in it. A barbecue favorite.

Saucisse is a moist, soft sausage that must be cooked before eating. You must refrigerate it and be aware of its shelf life. You'll usually be using it as an ingredient in recipes.

Saucisse Chorizo is sold fresh, cured, or smoked. It is a spicy pork sausage flavored with paprika and garlic whose origins reach from France to Spain.

Saucisse de Foie is a liver sausage, mostly pork liver. It is similar to liverwurst. It can be part of a plate of cold cuts.

Saucisson de Lyon must be cooked. It's wonderful on a bed of lentils or wrapped in brioche.

Saucisse de Montbéliard is usually cooked in boiling water. It comes from Franche-Comté and is smaller, less smoky, and not quite as fatty as the *saucisse de Morteau.*

Saucisse de Morteau is a smoked sausage from Franche-Comté in the eastern part of France. It is governed by IGP (Indication Géographique Protégée), which is a similar program to the AOC for French wines and cheeses. The designation dictates that it must be produced in a certain way. You'll usually find it cooked. A small piece of wood called a *cheville* is used to close it on one end.

Saucisse de Strasbourg and ***Saucisse de Francfort*** look and taste a lot like hot dogs. They are often used for dishes like *choucroute sarnie,* which features sauerkraut or pickled cabbage served with potatoes and meat.

Saucisse de Toulouse is usually one of the ingredients for the quintessential French bean dish, cassoulet. It is also excellent for pan frying.

Saucisson Sec is cured sausage that is dry enough to be sliced thin. Until you slice it, it doesn't need to be refrigerated. You'll enjoy this kind of sausage on an hors d'oeuvre tray with olives and fruits.

BEEF (*Boeuf*)

LOOKING AT ALL the beautiful cattle roaming the picturesque pastures in the French countryside just might make you hungry for beef. Deborah serves up two exquisite recipes—one for a quick and delicious steak dinner and the other for a hearty stew you'll love to come home to for a comforting, cocooning evening.

Hanger Steak (*Onglet*) with Sautéed Mushrooms (*Cépes*), Cream, and Brandy

—— SERVES 4 ——

This dish is rich and decadent,
perfect for visitors or for a special occasion.

INGREDIENTS

4 *onglet* steaks (or filet if you prefer)
Salt
Pepper
5 tablespoons (75 ml) butter, divided
1 tablespoon (15 ml) vegetable oil
2 pounds (900 g) *cépes* (small brown mushrooms), halved
2 cloves garlic, crushed and chopped
1 teaspoon (5 g) finely minced fresh thyme
¼ cup (60 ml) brandy
½ cup (125 ml) cream

EQUIPMENT

Knife for slicing
Large sauté pan
Measuring cups and spoons

Continued

Method

1. Season steaks with salt and pepper.
2. In a sauté pan, heat 1 tablespoon (15 ml) of the butter and the oil until bubbling and hot. Sear the steaks 2 to 3 minutes on each side. Don't keep turning them—you want to get good color so only one turn is necessary. The goal for this kind of steak is to cook it no more than medium rare.
3. Take the steaks out of the pan and put aside to rest.
4. Put the pan back on the stove and, still on high heat, add 2 table-spoons (30 ml) of the butter. Add half of the mushrooms when the butter is bubbling. Make sure not to overcrowd the mushrooms or they won't brown. When they are golden, remove them to a plate and repeat with the rest of the mushrooms.
5. When the next batch are golden, add the other mushrooms back to the pan as well as the garlic and thyme.
6. Season with salt and pepper, deglaze with the brandy, lower heat to medium, and let the mixture reduce by half. Stir for an additional minute.
7. Add the cream and let it simmer a minute or so while you slice and plate the steaks.
8. Cut the steaks across the grain into finger-wide slices. Arrange on a platter. Spoon mushrooms onto the platter and drizzle the sauce.

Pairing   Red Bordeaux

Variations, Ideas, Suggestions   Serve with a platter of oven-roasted asparagus.

If the cream is too rich for you, substitute 1 cup (250 ml) low-sodium beef broth, reduce by half, and finish with a tablespoon (15 ml) butter.

Beef (*Boeuf*) Bourguignon

Deborah's grandmother used to make this dish from Julia Child's cookbook, and everyone would swoon. It had fallen out of her repertoire until a friend served it for a party. The next day, Deborah called and begged him for his recipe. When he told her it was Julia Child's, she knew exactly why she loved it so much.
Here is Deborah's simplified, flourless version. If possible, make this the day before because it's even better after it has rested in the braising juices overnight.

INGREDIENTS

3 pounds (1.5 kg) beef chuck roast or brisket (*paleron, macreuse,* or *jumeau*), trimmed and cut into 2-inch (50 mm) chunks
Salt
Pepper
6 ounces (170 g) *lardons* or bacon, coarsely chopped
20 pearl onions
2 carrots, cut into ½-inch (13 mm) pieces
1 pound (450 g) mushrooms, quartered
3 tablespoons (45 ml) butter, more if needed

1 tablespoon (15 ml) olive oil, more if needed
1 medium onion, coarsely chopped
2 tablespoons (30 ml) tomato paste
4 cloves garlic, minced
½ bottle (375 ml) red wine
Herbs (2 parsley sprigs, 2 thyme sprigs, 2 bay leaves) tied together, so you can fish them out later
2 cups good quality beef stock, more if needed

EQUIPMENT

Dutch oven or large pot with lid
Knife for chopping and slicing
Slotted spoon or slotted spatula

Method

1. Pat the beef dry and season with salt and pepper. In a Dutch oven, cook bacon over medium heat until crispy. Fish the bacon out, leaving the grease, and set aside.

Continued

2. Increase the heat to medium high and brown the beef pieces on all sides. Do not overcrowd the meat in the pan. There must be a bit of space between each piece. Otherwise, the meat will not brown as the steam will not be able to escape. Therefore, you may have to brown the meat in batches. Use some oil if you need to.

3. After all the meat has been browned and removed from the pot, sauté the pearl onions, carrots, and mushrooms separately until golden, using the butter (use more butter if necessary). Remove from the pot, keeping them separated. Season with salt and pepper.

4. Add oil to the pot and when hot, add the onion to the pot, lowering the heat to medium. Sauté until softened. Then add the tomato paste and garlic, stirring about a minute, until fragrant.

5. Add the *lardons*, beef, wine, herbs, and stock to the pot. The beef should be just covered with the liquid. If not, add a little more stock. Add the pearl onions.

6. At this point, you can either put it in a preheated 350°F (175°C) oven for 3 to 4 hours or simmer on the stove on low about 2 hours. Make sure to put the lid on.

7. Halfway through cooking, add the carrots. When you have about 15 minutes left, add the mushrooms and leave the lid off to thicken the sauce a bit. The meat should be pretty much falling apart. Fish out the herbs.

8. Serve in bowls with crusty bread with a lovely green salad on the side.

Pairing   A rich Pinot Noir or a Rhône blend are good choices.

Variations, Ideas, Suggestions   Sometimes we roast cubed potatoes tossed in olive oil or butter in the oven until they are golden and crispy, and then throw them in when the carrots are added.

PORK (*Porc*)

PORK IS ONE of the most versatile meats. Its mild flavor blends with almost any cuisine, and it can be cooked with almost any method! You'll find recognizable, yummy cuts in every meat case. Deborah's pork loin with apples and onions is comfort food brought to a whole new level.

Pork Loin (*Longe de Porc*) with Apples (*Pommes*) and Onions

—— SERVES 4 ——

We think that the sign of an accomplished cook is his or her ability to take simple ingredients and prepare them perfectly. This recipe will make you the hero of the evening anywhere in the world you cook it for your family or guests. Add this fail-safe gem to your repertoire and shine every time.

INGREDIENTS

Salt
Pepper
1 pork tenderloin roast—about 1½ pounds (680 g) silver skin removed
4 cups (950 ml) apple juice or cider, reduced to about ½ cup (80 ml) or until syrupy
2 tablespoons (30 g) minced thyme
1 tablespoon (5 g) rosemary, minced
2 tablespoons (30 ml) Dijon mustard
6 tablespoons (90 ml) butter
20 pearl onions
3 tart apples, cored and quartered
2 tablespoons (30 ml) olive oil
¼ cup (60 ml) apple juice
¾ cup (375 ml) hard cider

EQUIPMENT

Knife for chopping and slicing
Measuring cups and spoons
Meat thermometer (optional)
Roasting pan

Method

1. Preheat oven to 350°F (175°C).
2. Salt and pepper the tenderloin. Mix together the apple reduction, thyme, rosemary, and mustard. Rub over the pork in a roasting pan. Dot with butter.

3. Toss onions and apple quarters with salt, pepper, and olive oil. Arrange around the pork.

4. Roast until 145°F (63°C) inside, 25 to 30 minutes.

5. Remove pan from oven and put the pork, apples, and onions on a platter and let rest about 10 minutes, tented with foil.

6. While the pork is resting, immediately put the roasting pan on a burner, add the ¼ cup apple juice and ¾ cup hard cider and turn the heat up high, quickly reducing to a sauce.

7. Slice pork into desired thickness, serve on the platter with the onions and apples scattered around the pork. Drizzle the sauce over the pork. Sprinkle with thyme leaves or sprigs.

Pairing   Hard cider or Pinot Gris

Variations, Ideas, Suggestions

• If you don't have a meat thermometer, try the old-fashioned way and use the touch method. When touched, raw meat has a mushy feeling. When it's firm, it's well done. You want pork cooked somewhere in between, but on the firmer side. If you are unsure at first, and you think your meat is done, make a small cut in the middle and use your eyes. And remember, when it rests, it will keep cooking a tiny bit more. Pork is perfect when it's still a little pink in the center. Almost no one likes dry meat.

• If you have a larger crowd, choose a pork loin instead of the smaller tenderloin and adjust the cooking time and ingredients.

LAMB (*Agneau*)

IT'S HARD FOR ME to understand how anyone could not love lamb. This dish is so delicious that I think it might even convert vegetarians.

Mead and Honey Braised Lamb Shanks (*Souris d'Agneau*)

——— SERVES 4 ———

This dish is even better the next day. And just so that you're aware, lamb shanks in France are not as large as they are in the United States.

INGREDIENTS

Salt
Pepper
4 small lamb shanks
1 tablespoon (5 g) finely minced fresh rosemary
4 tablespoons (60 ml) olive oil, divided
4 tablespoons (60 ml) butter
4 cloves garlic, minced
4 shallots, minced
2 cups (½ L) mead
2 cups (½ L) rich beef stock
¼ cup (60 ml) honey
1 sprig thyme

EQUIPMENT

Oven
Measuring cups and spoons
Ovenproof pot with lid

Method

1. Preheat oven to 275°F (135°C). Salt and pepper the lamb shanks.
2. Mix rosemary with 2 tablespoons (30 ml) of the olive oil and rub all over the shanks.

3. In an ovenproof pot with lid, melt the butter and add the remaining two tablespoons olive oil.

4. Over medium-high heat, brown the shanks on all sides. Don't crowd them or they won't brown. Remove shanks from the pan and set aside.

5. In the same pot, sauté garlic and shallots in the pan juices until fragrant. Add the shanks back to the pot, add the mead and enough beef stock to barely cover. Stir in the honey and add the thyme.

6. Braise for about 3 to 4 hours, or until the meat is loosening from the bone. Check once every hour and add more beef stock if necessary.

7. Before serving, remove shanks from the braising liquid, and reduce the liquid by about half.

8. Add the shanks back to the pot and simmer with reduced braising liquid on very low heat until heated through.

9. This is great served with the Pearl Couscous from the poultry chapter (see page 135). Spoon the sauce over. Enjoy!

Pairing   Red Rhône or mead from northwestern France

Variations, Ideas, Suggestions   If you don't have a reliable oven, you can braise this on the stove top. Simmer on low for about the same amount of time. If you don't have a lid for the simmer, just use a plate that is a bit larger than the pot. If you are low on mead, feel free to substitute with white wine or beer.

SAUSAGE—DRY OR COOKED
(*Saucisse; Saucisson*)

THE HUGE VARIETY of sausages in Europe has always fascinated me. Every country has its own specialties, and I have learned to love blood sausage and other mystery meats that I had never encountered in the United States. Be sure to try as many of them as you can while you are in France.

Lentils (*Lentilles*) with Andouille and Vinaigrette

—— SERVES 4 ——

A wonderful, very French-feeling dish for a picnic or lunch.

INGREDIENTS

2 whole andouille sausages (about
½ pound; 225 g) or *saucisson de
Lyon*
1 tablespoon (15 ml) olive oil
8 ounces (225 g) beluga or *du Puy*
lentils, rinsed
3 sprigs thyme
2 cups (½ L) chicken stock
2 cups (½ L) water
Salt
Pepper
2 teaspoons (10 ml) red wine
vinegar
Pinch of very finely minced
rosemary
½ small red onion, or small shallot,
finely diced
1 tablespoon (15 g) chopped parsley
2 tablespoons (30 ml) (or to taste)
Dijon Vinaigrette (see page 198)

EQUIPMENT

Large pot
Large sauté pan
Knife for dicing and chopping
Measuring spoon
Strainer (optional)

Method

1. Cut the sausages into ¼-inch (6 mm) slices.
2. If using cooked sausages, heat the olive oil in a large sauté pan and
   sauté the sausages on medium heat until lightly browned. Set aside
   and let cool. If using raw sausages, make sure to cook the sausage
   slices all the way through. You may need a little more oil.

3. Put lentils and thyme in a large pot and add the chicken stock and water to cover by 2 inches (5 cm). Bring to a boil, then reduce heat and simmer gently for about 30 minutes for beluga lentils and about 45 minutes for *du Puy* lentils. Do not overcook or boil too rapidly, as they will turn to mush. Then you will need to make soup instead of this dish! They should be tender yet firm and not mushy when finished.

4. Strain off any remaining liquid and spread out the lentils on a sheet pan (or a large plate or platter) to cool so they don't keep cooking. You want the steam to be released. Season with salt and pepper and red wine vinegar and the rosemary while they are still warm. Toss to distribute. Pick out thyme when it is cool enough to touch.

5. Toss the cooled lentils with the raw red onion, parsley, sliced andouille, and vinaigrette.

6. Can be served warm or room temperature.

Pairing   Red Rhône blend or Corbières

Variations, Ideas, Suggestions

- Try substituting warmed leftover lamb, guinea fowl, or duck. Add chopped arugula to the chilled lentils for a lighter dish.
- Omit the sausage for a vegetarian dish.
- Omit sausage, vinaigrette, parsley, and onion and serve as a hot side dish.

MEATY FRENCH FESTIVALS

Provided you are not a card-carrying vegetarian, the many meat-related festivals the French enjoy may be just the destination for you! Here is a short list of some of the celebrations you might want to attend.

La Foire au Jambon **(Bayonne Ham Fair):** Bayonne ham has been appreciated since the Middle Ages, and over the Easter holiday weekend more than thirty local producers offer tastes of their products to revelers at the fair in this southwestern city. There are dozens of sporting and culinary contests and plenty of good food, drink, and dancing to enjoy.

Spring Lamb and Claret: Pauillac, a small village and port in the Médoc region, has the distinction of hosting three of the five "first growths" in the 1855 classification of Bordeaux wines. There is a banquet, sheep dog demos, "meet the sheep," sheep shearing, a spring market, boat trips, an art exhibition, and a chance to buy a beret! Lamb is a specialty of the region since there are marshy areas near the river that are totally unsuitable for vines but are excellent for rearing salt marsh lamb.

Andouille Festival: The town of Aire-sur-la-Lys, in Nord-Pas-de-Calais-Picardie, claims that its artisanal sausage was created in the nineteenth century. The first weekend in September, this pork meat/pork stomach concoction is celebrated with a festival that includes a colorful parade, concerts, dancing, and of course, abundant opportunities for dining and wine tasting.

Goat Meat Eaters' Fête: A feast, with goat meat as its focus, is enjoyed by all in attendance. If you're near Clermont-Ferrand or Limoges, it might just be worth a visit.

La Frairie des Petits Ventres **(The Brotherhood of Small Bellies):** This annual event held in Limoges dates back to the year 930 AD. The city's butchers take to the street to show off their specialty meats. A celebrated dish at the festival is *amourettes*, a dish of sheep testicles cooked in garlic, parsley, and port. Organ meats like sweetbreads, tripe, and the organs of lamb, veal, and pigs are the stars of this one-day festival.

Chapter 8

FISH AND
SHELLFISH

(Poisson et Fruits de Mer)

"What a flavor oysters have—
mellow, coppery, with almost
a creaminess when you
chew and analyze.
I drank some good beer
with them and floated on a
gastronomically sensual cloud."

———

JAMES BEARD

Recipes featured in this chapter:

Seared Scallops (Coquilles Saint-Jacques) *with*
Peas (Pois), *Bacon, and Mint* (Menthe)
Lobster (Homard) *à l'Armoricaine*
Simple Shellfish (Fruits de Mer) *Bouillabaisse*
Crab (Crabe), *Lamb's Lettuce* (Mâche), *and Avocado*
(Avocat) *with Grapefruit* (Pamplemousse) *Vinaigrette*
Seared Salmon (Saumon) *with Fennel* (Fenouil), *Olives, and Orange*

A s we were swooning over a fabulous meal of crêpes with our dear friends Andie and Georges in Paris one evening, talk turned to travel in Northwest France. Tim and I had never been there, but after they told us that Normandy was the source of France's best mussels, oysters, and scallops, we were ready to pack up and go that minute! A plan was born, and a few days later we crammed into their little blue Peugeot and drove about three hours to the northwest of France. It was a brilliantly sunny day, and the scenery, once we left the freeway, was gorgeously French. Fat cattle lazing under ancient trees trembling in the breeze, gorgeous châteaux with ornate gates guarding tree-lined drives and gardens, and rolling pastures where horses grazed swept past our windows.

Honfleur sparkled in the midday sun. The harbor town has been a transit port and a reliable source of seafood since the twelfth century. Gorgeous yachts awaited their owners' next outing, and tourists strolled and snapped photos along cobblestone lanes. Tall, slate-covered, storybook houses stood shoulder to shoulder along the quay, and sidewalk cafés with colorful awnings, with their menus written in chalk on sandwich boards, beckoned to us. The billboards offered shrimp, lobster, conch, periwinkle, mussels, and, of course, oysters prepared every way imaginable. We chose a café in a shady spot with a view of the busy harbor where we toasted our good fortune and friendship with crisp rosé.

Even in tourist areas, French meals proceed at a leisurely pace, and we slowly worked our way through several courses on that lazy afternoon. The oysters on the half shell, piled on platters of coarse salt, were so fresh that they quivered when we squirted them with lemon juice. Next, we feasted on individual cauldrons of tender mussels and sopped up the herbed liquor with chunks of crusty bread. Crisp *frites* appeared in wire cones lined with greasy paper.

When the waiter removed the mountain of mussel shells from the center of the table, we settled back in our shady corner to share more stories and laughter. It was an afternoon I hoped would never end.

After lunch, we drove into the countryside in search of our B&B and we were thrilled when we saw the long driveway, lined with imposing old trees, leading to a graceful two-story gray stone mansion. French blue shutters framed windows with billowing white curtains. We were to spend several nights in this dreamy setting.

We toured the beaches of the Normandy invasion by day, stopping at every village's farmers' market, where Andie would chat with the cheese and butter makers and then translate for us. They scooped creamy butter out of tubs and then patted it by hand into rectangular shapes for the customers, wrapping and weighing each package as it was sold. The fresh-caught wares from local fishermen rested on beds of ice, and we slurped the briny oyster samples they offered. The best and closest market to our digs was in Saint-Lô. The stalls and colorful umbrellas of the market sprawled through the whole town. In the nearby town of Torigni-sur-Vire there's a market on Monday mornings that includes livestock auctions. Pigs, cows, calves, bulls, and sheep come under the auctioneer's hammer there every week.

Each night we dined in a different nearby country town. Our B&B host at La Beauconniere, a hilarious Englishman, entertained us every evening at the cocktail hour with his outrageous stories, and he made reservations each day for us in nearby family-run restaurants. We would never have discovered these out-of-the-way gems on our own. Every one of them was cozy and quaint with a welcoming open fireplace, and their cheerful staffs made us feel as if we were dinner guests in a French home. Our dinners lasted for hours as we devoured local mussels, oysters, scallops, and lamb. We kibitzed with waitstaff (usually sons and daughters of the owner), and enjoyed reliving the day's adventures as we dined. We were thrilled with the high quality of ingredients and creative talents of those excellent chefs. And, of course, superb French wine elevated our experience with every sip.

The last morning we filled an ice chest with our treasured butter treats and shellfish from that morning's catch into Andie's tiny Peugeot, and back to Paris we went. We had so much fun that on the return trip we began to plan our next adventure—to the South of France, where bouillabaisse originated and the Côte d'Azur basked in its Mediterranean sunshine.

WHERE TO SHOP FOR FISH

Of course, the optimum fish-shopping experience is right at the harbor where the gulls swoop, the riggings slap against the sailboats' masts, and fishermen in rubber boots and aprons hurl their catch onto tables where they'll prepare your order before your eyes. Places like Villefranche-sur-Mer or Toulon in the South of France or Calais or Deauville on the Atlantic Coast are among the more than 50 seaports where the country's seafood first hits its shores. Freshwater fish like trout or bream are plentiful too, and fish can be purchased at almost every farmers' market in the country. There are also fish shops in most towns where proprietors put their fish bins right on the sidewalk with their wares nestled in huge piles of shaved ice. Even the *supermarché* offers fish in their cold shelves, but it's so easy to find genuine fishmongers who can offer advice and prepare your fish to order that you really should make the effort to buy it at a shop.

If you're in Marseille, you can get all the fish you could dream of at the picturesque Le Marché de la Pêche. This outdoor fish market is held every morning from 8 a.m. to 1 p.m., and you'll be rubbing shoulders with local restaurateurs as they choose their ingredients for the day. You can find the catch of the day fresh off the boat: red mullet, bream, grouper, and more. They'll weigh and clean it for you while you wait. If you want an even more exciting fish experience, you can visit the wholesale fish market. It's in Saumaty on the road toward the town of L'Estaque. You can get there on the 35 bus. Not far from the fish market is Les Halles de la Major, a bustling covered food market where you'll find high-end regional produce, meat, fish, herbs, and a tapas bar. It's right next to the Musée Regards de Provence.

HOW TO SHOP FOR THE RIGHT FISH

When you've decided to take the plunge and interact with a real French fishmonger instead of grabbing a plastic tray from the *supermarché,* take your time and pay attention to the shop's clientele. Whether you're at the farmers' market, at the harbor, or a shop in town, the place with the longest line of waiting customers is sure to have the best reputation. Also, a lot of traffic means that the fish is moving

out quickly, and chances are it hasn't been languishing in a case for a day or two.

Fresh fish should look almost alive. Their eyes will be bright and clear, and the flesh firm to the touch. The fish should smell sweet, too, like fresh ocean air. Any fishy odor means the fish is just not fresh enough.

SHELLFISH (*Fruits de Mer*)

The nose knows! If you smell ammonia, skip the shellfish and change your menu. If you're cooking bivalves, like clams, oysters, mussels, or scallops, do not purchase any that are open. Toss any that do not open after cooking. Be sure to look for shell damage. If an oyster shell is chipped, cracked, or open, don't buy it. When you tap the shell, if it's alive, it should tighten up. When shucked, the oyster meat should be pale, plump, and glossy. If it's a dull tan color, discard it. But if it's green, dig in. The greenish color of *verte* oysters comes from a particular type of blue diatom (a type of single-celled algae) that those oysters eat. It's sought after in France so grab some if you find them. We can teach you how to shuck oysters on page 42.

Scallop season in Northwest France is from October 1st to the end of May. They come live in the shell, so all the rules of shellfish freshness apply. If you are worried about trying to shuck your scallops, ask your fishmonger to do it for you.

Since they are usually alive when you purchase them, scallops come with their coral, or roe, attached. We don't see this often in America because the coral is highly perishable and is discarded in processing. That's a shame because it's tart and delicious, although it's an acquired taste for some. You can cook the scallops with the roe still attached, or you can detach it and cook it separately to use as a beautiful coral garnish.

Many Americans avoid scallops because they've only eaten overcooked, rubbery renditions. It's all in the preparation. When cooking them, rely on the touch test. If they are mushy, they are undercooked. If they are firm, they are overcooked. If you follow Deborah's instructions carefully, you'll achieve the perfect doneness, and you'll be a scallop fan forever.

STORAGE

Ideally, you should buy fish the day you're going to cook it, but sometimes life gets in the way. Say you receive a glamorous dinner invitation that you simply can't resist and that fish you just brought home is staring at you with its bright, glassy eyes, giving you guilt for not doing something with it. Because fish is one of the most perishable ingredients on the planet, you need to find a way to preserve it without ruining its delicate flavor, freshness, and texture.

Here's your solution: Rinse and dry the fish, and then place it in a single layer in a large sealable plastic bag. Put a bed of ice on a pan, put the fish on top, and cover with more ice. The goal is to keep the fish as cold and as dry as possible. The bacteria that spoils fish thrives in moisture.

Put the pan on the bottom shelf of the refrigerator. Don't skimp on the ice. If your pan is too shallow and you're worried that melted ice will spill all over your fridge, put the ice in plastic sealable bags as well.

Even with these storage precautions, you should cook and eat the fish within two days. Remember that not all types of fish spoil equally. The oilier the fish, the faster it goes off.

When storing oysters and other live shellfish, do not seal them in plastic as you would other fish because they are alive, and doing this will probably kill the poor things. Put them on ice and cover them with a moist towel. They will keep well chilled for a maximum of two days in your refrigerator.

ABOUT LOBSTER

Buying Lobster: There are hard and softshell lobsters. If the shell is a little soft, it means that the lobster has recently shed its hard carapace and so the meat will be a bit sweeter. If you can get a look at the underbelly, it should be bright red, as should the claws. A clean shell without marks and scrapes means it's soft. Most important: Live lobsters should have *no* odor.

The Fish You'll Find in France

Bream: *la daurade*

Cod: *la morue*

Clam: *le clam*

Cockle: *la coque*

Crab: *le crabe*

Crayfish: *l'écrevisse*

Cuttlefish: *la seiche*

Haddock: *l'aiglefin*

Halibut: *le flétan*

Lobster: *l'homard*

Langoustine: *la langoustine* (This tastes like a cross between a small lobster and a shrimp.)

Mackerel: *la maquereau*

Monkfish: *la lotte*

Mussel: *la moule*

Octopus: *la pieuvre*

Oyster: *l'huître*

Razor shell: *le couteau*

Salmon: *la saumon*

Sardine: *la sardine*

Scallop: *la coquille Saint-Jacques*

Sea bass: *le bar*

Shrimp/prawn: *la crevette*

Skate: *la raie*

Squid: *le calmar*

Swordfish: *l'espadon*

Trout: *la truite*

Tuna: *le thon*

Whiting: *le merlan*

Fishy Terms

Bone: *l'arête*

Boned: *sans l'arête*

Cleaned: *préparé*

Fillet: *le filet*

Filleted: *en filets*

Fresh: *frais*

Frozen: *surgelé*

Ice: *la glace*

Loin: *la longe*

Salted: *salé*

Scaled: *écaille*

Skinned: *sans peau*

Smoked: *fumé*

Steak: *la tranche*

Tail: *la queue*

SHELLFISH *(Fruits de Mer)*

DEBORAH'S SIMPLE but tasty recipe for Lobster (*Homard*) à l'Armoricaine (see page 179) takes me back to Normandy's La Marée restaurant, which has been serving dinners in Grandcamp-Maisy, right by Pointe du Hoc, for 70 years.

Seared Scallops (*Coquilles Saint-Jacques*) with Peas (*Pois*), Bacon, and Mint (*Menthe*)

—— SERVES 4 ——

In the sixties, I attended college in Oklahoma. A chef courageously opened the city's first French restaurant and I was thrilled to accept an invitation. A waiter sporting a long apron and a Gallic accent, either of which may or may not have been authentic, served me coquilles Saint-Jacques *presented in a real shell. In an instant, I was hopelessly hooked on what was then called "continental" cuisine. The elegance of French dining, even in an Oklahoma strip mall, made an indelible impression. Preparing Deborah's beautiful recipe always transports me back to that memorable meal.*

INGREDIENTS

8 large fresh sea scallops (two per person)
Sea salt
Pepper
1½ cups (375 ml) fresh or frozen peas
2 pieces of bacon, cut into ¼-inch (6 mm) pieces, or *lardons*
1 shallot, roughly chopped
1 teaspoon (5 ml) lemon juice
Piment d'espelette or paprika to taste
2 tablespoons (30 g) minced fresh mint

EQUIPMENT

Knife for chopping
Large sauté pan
Measuring cups and spoons
Strainer (or see *Variations, Ideas, Suggestions*)

Continued

Method

1. Blot the scallops on both sides with a paper towel to dry. Salt and pepper them. In a sauté pan, simmer the fresh or still frozen peas in lightly salted water until just tender. Be careful not to overcook. You don't want them to turn dark green because they will be mushy and will have lost their bright flavor. Strain and set aside.

2. Wipe the moisture out of the pan and over medium heat, sauté the bacon until the fat starts to render. Add the shallots. Reduce heat to medium-low and cook until the bacon is brown and the shallots are nicely caramelized. Fish the bacon and shallots out of the pan and add to the peas. Season the pea mixture with salt, lemon juice, *piment d'espelette*, and half of the mint.

3. With the grease still in the pan, turn the heat to high. When it's very hot and smoking a bit, add the scallops, making sure they are not touching. Sear them about 2 minutes on each side. Don't overcook. They should be brown on the outside and still translucent in the very center. If they don't all fit in the pan, then sear them in two batches.

4. Put two scallops on each plate. Quickly toss the pea mixture into the pan to reheat for a few seconds. Spoon the mixture over the scallops and sprinkle with more mint.

Pairing   Semillon-Sauvignon Blend or Muscadet

Variations, Ideas, Suggestions

- It's almost impossible to find fresh peas unless you go to the farm the day they are picked or grow them yourself. So there is no shame in purchasing good quality frozen ones. Make sure they are small and bright green.
- If you don't have a strainer, use a cheese grater against the edge of the tilted pot or pan to catch the peas as you release the water.

Lobster (*Homard*) à l'Armoricaine

—— SERVES 4 ——

This is an appetizer portion of a classic dish from France's northwest. While the name might seem to reference America, and most people actually call the sauce Américaine, it is thought to be derived from Armorica, the ancient name for the northwestern part of France, which means "place by the sea."

INGREDIENTS

4 tablespoons (60 ml) plus 2 tablespoons (30 ml) butter, divided
1 tablespoon (15 ml) olive oil
1 shallot, minced
2 cloves garlic, minced
1 cup (250 ml) mead or white wine
2 medium heirloom tomatoes,
  chopped into small pieces, or
  one 14-ounce (450 ml) can of
  good quality crushed tomatoes
¾ cup (180 ml) fish or chicken
  stock
1 tablespoon (15 g) finely chopped
  parsley
1 teaspoon (5 g) finely chopped
  thyme
2 tablespoons (30 g) finely chopped
  tarragon, divided
¼ teaspoon (1.5 g) *piment
  d'espelette* or paprika or cayenne
4 small *homards* (lobsters), removed
  from the shells (ask your fishmonger to do this, but if your
  French doesn't stretch that far,
  try the time-honored method of
  pantomime)

2 ounces (60 ml) Calvados or
  Cognac
¼ cup (62 ml) cream
1 teaspoon (5 ml) pastis (optional)
Salt
Pepper

EQUIPMENT

Knife for chopping
Large sauté pan
Measuring cups and spoons
Medium sauté pan
Sieve or mesh strainer (optional)

Continued

Method

1. Melt the butter and oil in a large sauté pan. Add the shallots and garlic and cook on medium heat until lightly caramelized, about 10 minutes. Deglaze with the mead.

2. Add the tomatoes and simmer for 10 minutes until the liquid is reduced by about half.

3. Add the stock, parsley, thyme, half of the tarragon, and the *piment d'espelette* to the pan and simmer about 15 minutes, until reduced and thickened a bit. Strain the sauce into another saucepan, pushing on the solids. This results in a more refined dish. Or just keep it rustic and continue!

4. In a medium sauté pan, add 2 tablespoons (30 ml) of butter on medium-high heat. When bubbling, add the lobster meat and sauté on each side until pink and the tails start to curl. Do not cook all the way through. Deglaze with the Calvados.

5. Scrape the lobster, Calvados, and any other pan juices and bits into the sauce. Add cream and the pastis if using and let simmer on low about another 5 minutes, until the lobster is just done. Taste and add salt and pepper as necessary. Don't season until the end, though, as the lobster and the stock will probably be salty enough.

6. Serve in a bowl with the remaining tarragon and crusty bread.

Pairing   Tavel Rosé or Bandol Rosé

TIP: *To remove the lobster meat from the shell: Bring a pot of lightly salted water (large enough to fit the lobster tails) to a boil. Place the lobster in the water and simmer until they are just beginning to curl. Do not cook them all the way. Remove and rinse with cold water. With scissors, cut along the bottom side or belly side of the lobster. Split open the tail and remove the meat. Remove the claw meat by cracking them with a mallet or the back of a large knife first. Don't forget the joints.*

Simple Shellfish (*Fruits de Mer*) Bouillabaisse

This recipe is a simplified version of a traditional Provençal fish stew that originated in that exotic city, Marseille. Don't let the long list of ingredients intimidate you. It's really effortless to assemble and so satisfying that you'll make it often. Here's what to do when you come home from the fish market.

INGREDIENTS

3 tablespoons (45 ml) olive oil or vegetable oil
1 large onion, thinly sliced
6 cloves garlic, smashed and chopped
1 small fennel bulb, thinly sliced
½ cup (125 ml) dry white wine
One 14-ounce (450 ml) can of whole, peeled tomatoes with juice, or 4 large in-season ripe tomatoes, cored and roughly chopped
6 cups (1.5 L) seafood stock, or 3 cups (.75 L) clam juice and 3 cups (.75 L) chicken or vegetable stock
1 strip orange zest
4 tablespoons (30 ml) orange juice
¼ teaspoon (1 g) saffron, or ½ teaspoon (2 g) paprika
2 pounds (900 g) fresh clams or cockles
1 pound (450 g) shrimp or langoustine, peeled
1 pound (450 g) mussels
Sea salt
1 bunch parsley, chopped
4 to 6 tablespoons (60–90 ml) rouille (optional)
1 lemon, cut into six wedges

EQUIPMENT

Can opener (optional)
Knife for slicing and chopping
Large heavy pot
Measuring cups and spoons
Paring knife

Method

1. Heat the oil in a large heavy pot. Sauté onion, garlic, and fennel over medium heat until light golden brown, about 8 minutes or so. Pour in white wine to deglaze.

Continued

2. Add the tomatoes, stock, zest, orange juice, and saffron and bring to a boil, simmering on a light boil until the liquid reduces by about half. This will take between 15 and 20 minutes.

3. Add shellfish and cook until the shells are open. Discard any shellfish that didn't open. Fish out the orange peel. Taste and add salt only if needed.

4. Serve in bowls and top with parsley and rouille, if using, plus a lemon wedge on the side.

5. Serve with a baguette, of course!

Pairing   A dry rosé from Provence or a Sauvignon Blanc

Variations, Ideas, Suggestions

- Feel free to substitute any of the shellfish with another kind of fish. If you are adding other fish, cut it into chunks and add it after the shellfish has been in the pot for about 2 minutes.
- Rouille, a sauce or condiment consisting of olive oil, breadcrumbs, garlic, saffron, and cayenne pepper, is available in jars for you to purchase, or if you have lots of time and patience, you can make it yourself.
- Saffron is traditional in bouillabaisse but very expensive. Even though some people will say it's not bouillabaisse without the saffron, don't worry if you leave it out. It will still be delicious.

Crab (*Crabe*), Lamb's Lettuce (*Mâche*), and Avocado (*Avocat*) with Grapefruit (*Pamplemousse*) Vinaigrette

—— SERVES 4 ——

Crab is available almost everywhere in France, but buying it fresh from the fishermen on the Côte d'Azur will make it taste even better. Here's a tip about buying crab: avoid fresh-picked crabmeat that smells off in any way. Blueing, a term that describes when pockets of blue or gray form in the meat, can happen with previously frozen crab that wasn't stored properly. In this case, the texture and flavor will suffer. Assuming you're starting with wonderful, fresh-cooked crab, here's a simple, delicious way to prepare it.

INGREDIENTS

Vinaigrette
Makes about 1¼ cups (30 ml)

¼ cup (60 ml) juice from grapefruit of any color (preferably ruby)
1½ tablespoons (22 ml) cider vinegar or red wine vinegar
1 tablespoon (15 ml) honey
¼ cup (60 ml) olive oil
Sea salt
Pepper

Salad
1 pound (450 g) fresh-cooked crab meat, out of its shell from the fish vendor
3 green onions, roots removed and thinly sliced on the diagonal
2 cups (225 g) *mâche* (this tender lettuce with its tiny dark green leaves is beloved in France and can also be found in the United States in upscale markets)
1 ripe avocado, peeled, pitted, and cut into 12 wedges
¼ cup (32 g) crushed toasted hazelnuts
2 teaspoons (10 g) chopped tarragon

Knife for chopping and slicing
Measuring cups and spoons
Medium-sized bowl or salad bowl
Whisk

Method

1. For the vinaigrette: Whisk together all of the vinaigrette ingredients. Taste and adjust seasonings. Some grapefruits might be more tart than others so you may need more honey or oil, or if the grapefruit is mild, you may need more juice.
2. For the salad: Gently mix the crab with the green onion slices.
3. Toss the *mâche* with a couple tablespoons of the vinaigrette and place on four plates. Divide and arrange the avocado slices on the *mâche* and the crab in the middle. Drizzle with more dressing, about 2 tablespoons per plate. Sprinkle with hazelnuts and tarragon.

Variations, Ideas, Suggestions

- You can also include grapefruit sections in this salad if you have some left over after making the vinaigrette.
- Try this with seared scallops instead of crab.

FISH (*Poisson*)

SHOPPING FOR ANYTHING in France is an adventure for me, and although I revel in the beautiful displays of fruits and vegetables, herbs and poultry, it's the fishmongers' displays that thrill me the most. The incredibly fresh, glistening whole fish trying to make contact with their bright eyes, the octopus legs just waiting for the barbecue, the fat pink shrimps that will land on my hors d'oeuvre platter, always make me stop for a look.

Seared Salmon (*Saumon*) with Fennel (*Fenouil*), Olives, and Orange

—— SERVES 4 ——

The rich brininess of the olives and the sweet high notes of the orange complement each other and make the salmon stand out. This is an appetizer or light lunch. Just double everything if it's for dinner.

INGREDIENTS

1 tablespoon (15 ml) olive oil
1½ teaspoons (8 ml) vinegar
1½ teaspoons (8 ml) orange juice
1 pound (450 g) salmon, skin and
  bones removed
Sea salt
Pepper
1 orange, peeled and sliced
2 tablespoons (30 ml) vegetable oil,
  divided
2 tablespoons (30 ml) butter,
  divided
1 head fennel, trimmed and thinly
  sliced
8–12 olives, pitted and coarsely
  chopped (we suggest *lucques,*
  Picholine, or Niçoise)
2 teaspoons (10 ml) roughly
  chopped fennel fronds

EQUIPMENT

Knife for chopping and slicing
Large sauté pan
Measuring spoons

Method

1. Mix together the olive oil, vinegar, and orange juice.
2. Cut the salmon into four equal pieces. Season with salt and pepper. Cut orange slices in half.

Continued

3. In a sauté pan, heat 1 tablespoon (15 ml) of the oil and 1 tablespoon (15 ml) of the butter on high heat until bubbling. Sear the fennel about 1 minute on each side. Remove from pan and toss with orange slices, olives, and dressing.

4. Turn heat down on the pan to medium and add remaining oil and butter. Sprinkle salt in the pan and cook the salmon pieces about 3 minutes on each side. Check for doneness either by making a small incision in the center (the salmon should be pink and still somewhat translucent in the very center) or by pressing on the fish to check for firmness. Do not overcook.

5. Divide the fennel mixture onto four appetizer or salad-sized plates, top with salmon, and sprinkle with fennel fronds.

Pairing   Chenin Blanc or Pinot Noir

FISHY FRENCH FESTIVALS

Oyster Festival at Gujan-Mestras: This festival, held in August, takes place in a natural harbor that's just a short drive from Bordeaux. The Arcachon Bay oysters are particularly sumptuous.

La Fête de la Mer et du Maquereau: In September, the Côte Fleurie resort town of Trouville-sur-Mer in Normandy organizes a celebration of the sea over a weekend period. Enjoy mackerel tastings and sea shanties. On Sunday, in memory of fishermen lost at sea, there is a mass in the morning followed by a wreath-laying at sea. In the afternoon, boats give trips out to sea.

Boulogne-sur-Mer: Boulogne has long been France's largest fishing port, and the town plays host to an intriguing event that commemorates the Route du Poisson on which horse-drawn carts and fishmongers used to travel daily to take their fresh fish from Boulogne to Les Halles, the market in Paris. Every two years (even years) in July, this historic trip is celebrated. In November, the city also hosts a mackerel festival.

La Fête de la Coquille Saint-Jacques: The charming seaside resort on the Côte Fleurie, Villers-sur-Mer, celebrates the Coquille Saint-Jacques in October. A huge market sells the scallops, other seafood, and local products—all in a festive atmosphere.

La Fête de la Crevette: One of the few remaining old-style ports in Normandy, Honfleur, celebrates its lifeline to the sea with a large shrimp festival in early October. Of course, there'll be plenty of the little things available to eat, but who's going to peel them all? The organizers have cunningly arranged a shrimp-peeling competition so that visitors don't have to get their hands dirty.

La Fête du Hareng (Herring): In November, the town of Étaples celebrates the herring. Fishermen and cooks dressed in local costume serve the fish, which are available smoked or grilled. Packed with protein and goodness, they are extremely filling, so you'd do well to pace yourself.

Chapter 9

FRUITS AND VEGETABLES

(Fruits et Legumes)

"Life expectancy would
grow by leaps and bounds
if green vegetables
smelled as good as bacon."

———

DOUG LARSON

Recipes featured in this chapter:

Dijon Vinaigrette

*Chopped Endive, Blue Cheese, Persimmon (*Kaki*), and Walnut Salad*

*Roasted Garlic Artichoke (*Artichaut*)*

Tartiflette

*Oven-Roasted Haricots Verts or Asparagus (*Asperges*)*

Hazelnut Orange Persillade

*Roasted Cauliflower (*Chou-Fleur*) with Currants and Capers*

*Canteloupe (*Melon de Cavaillon*) with Bayonne Ham*

*(*Jambon de Bayonne*) and Toasted Almonds*

*Seared Persimmon (*Kaki*) with Fromage Blanc, Honey, and Truffle Salt*

The quality of fruits and vegetables in France is clearly evident in the extravagant displays at farmers' markets, the small mom-and-pop *magasins de légumes* (vegetable shops) found in almost every neighborhood, and local grocery stores. Although vegetables are usually supporting actors on the dinner plate, the French still choose and prepare them with the same care that they take with all their food. Since most French people shop often, they look for produce that's just at the perfect point of ripeness for the dish they're preparing.

There are food festivals all over France, especially in the warmer months, that celebrate many kinds of produce. One of our favorites is the truffles celebration in Sarlat-la-Canéda, an unforgettably pictur-esque town in the Périgord Noir region, which is thought to have been occupied since Gallo-Roman times. The area is known for truffles and geese (think pâté), and every January they celebrate with a weeklong truffle extravaganza. There are workshops on truffle identification, truffle hunting demonstrations with trained dogs, and of course tastings of the pricey fungi and its frequent companion, foie gras.

The French are supremely conscious of eating things that are actually in season locally, so strawberries in January are sure to be from outside the country. The following list from *Le Parisien* will help you plan your shopping trips, since it includes what you can expect to find in each season.

SEASONAL FRUITS AND VEGETABLES IN FRANCE

April: Starting to appear: rhubarb, blackberries, asparagus, chard, spinach, radishes, lettuce.

   Still in season: oranges, beets, carrots, celery, cabbage, endive, potatoes.

May: Starting to appear: strawberries, eggplants, cucumbers, turnips, cauliflower.

   Still in season: rhubarb, blackberries, asparagus, beets, carrots, celery, cabbage, spinach, radishes, potatoes, lettuce.

June: Starting to appear: apricots, cherries, currants, raspberries, melons, apples, tomatoes, zucchini, fennel, beans, leeks, peas, peppers.

   Still in season: rhubarb, blackberries, asparagus, beets, carrots, celery, cabbage, cauliflower, spinach, lettuce, turnips, onions, potatoes, radishes.

Summer: Continue to enjoy strawberries, the last cherries, and apricots. It's also still the high season for nectarines, peaches, plums, and pears. Grapes arrive. Zucchini, tomatoes, melons, beans, peppers, broccoli, and all lettuces are in abundance.

Fall: Enjoy grapes until October. Also, raspberries, blackberries, and blueberries are still available. You can find most summer veggies until November.

Winter: Apples and pears are everywhere. Oranges and clementines arrive in November. Now's the time to cook cabbages, carrots, potatoes, leeks, and endive.

POPULAR FRENCH VEGETABLES AND FRUITS

These are everyday produce, but are extremely popular in France.

Popular Vegetables

Poireaux (leeks)   *Oignons* (onions)
Haricots verts (small green beans)   *Aubergine* (eggplant)
Tomates (tomatoes)   *Courgettes* (zucchini)

Popular Fruits

Poires (pears)   *Raisins* (grapes)
Pommes (apples)   *Cerises* (cherries)

SPECIAL FRENCH VEGETABLES AND FRUITS

These are some special items you can find in France. In this food heaven, you can get almost anything.

Special Vegetables

Endive—a rocket-shaped white vegetable from Belgium with a nutty flavor.

Cèpes—a large, very tasty mushroom.

Porcini—a large, very tasty mushroom.

Morilles (morels)—these delicious fungi are found in many places around the world; they resemble a sponge.

Chanterelle—these sought-after mushrooms grow in the wild and are meaty, lily-shaped, and can be orange, yellow, or white.

Mâche—a salad green that is tender and has a slightly sweet taste.

Special Fruits

Kaki (persimmon)

Prune mirabelle (mirabelle plum)

Melon de Cavaillon (slightly smaller and sweeter than a cantaloupe)

HOW TO PREPARE THE PERFECT
FRENCH GREEN *SALADE*

In France, the salad course is served after the main course and before the cheese course. This salad can be your mainstay during your entire time in France. Here are the basic ingredients, but you can be as creative as you please.

Pick up some crisp, fresh salad greens at the market. Toss with homemade vinaigrette. Voilà! Simple salad, happy diners. Typical French salad greens would be either Boston lettuce, escarole, or *feuille de chene* (oak leaf), but do experiment with other seasonal greens you may find. Because this is such a simple dish, the quality of the ingredients is critical. So splurge on a bottle of excellent, unflavored olive oil and quality vinegar.

VEGETABLES (*Legumes*)

LILLIPUTIAN REFRIGERATORS are not the only reason that the French shop every day. Their appreciation of quality ingredients and the ready availability of truly fresh produce make shopping every day the sensible thing to do. Here Deborah shows us how to make the most of the lovely things you'll bring home from the market.

Dijon Vinaigrette

—— MAKES ABOUT ½ CUP (120 ML) ——

Vinaigrette is the staple French salad dressing. Its base of Dijon mustard and vinegar allows for almost endless variations from sweet to savory.

INGREDIENTS

1½ teaspoons (8 ml) Dijon
    mustard
3 tablespoons (45 ml) red wine
    vinegar
Pinch of sugar or a couple drops of
    honey, more if needed
Salt
Pepper
½ cup (120 ml) olive oil

EQUIPMENT

Bowl
Measuring cups and spoons
Whisk (optional)

Method

1. Mix all ingredients except the olive oil together in the bottom of a bowl. Then whisk in the oil, slowly.

Variations, Ideas, Suggestions

- If you don't have a whisk, use a fork. Or put all the ingredients in a jar with a lid and shake it.
- Enhance the dressing by adding crushed garlic or finely chopped shallot or fresh herbs or all of these.
- Improve the salad by adding snipped herbs, radish, or cucumber.
- Use scissors for the herbs—for some, it's easier to use than a knife and doesn't bruise the leaves as much.
- Try adding ½ tablespoon (8 ml) honey and then add some sliced apple, persimmon, or nuts to your salad.
- Make a much larger amount of dressing and keep it in a jar in the refrigerator to use during your stay.
- To avoid soggy greens and to achieve evenly coated leaves, drizzle the dressing around the edge of the salad bowl. Then add the greens and toss, letting them fluff up against the sides of the bowl to capture the dressing.
- Substitute the vinegar and mustard with fresh lemon juice and a bit of honey for a refreshing change.
- Try different types of vinegars.
- Add a tablespoon of Tahini Sauce (see page 50) to make a creamy dressing.

Chopped Endive, Blue Cheese, Persimmon (*Kaki*), and Walnut Salad

*Since this salad isn't likely to wilt too much before
you consume it, it's ideal for alfresco dining.*

INGREDIENTS

1 tablespoon (15 ml) honey
2 tablespoons (30 ml) cider vinegar
(or use what you have on hand)
2 tablespoons (30 ml) olive oil
3 heads of endive, sliced crosswise
in ½-inch (1.25 cm) pieces
(discard the end)
½ cup (125 ml) roughly chopped
toasted walnuts or pecans
4 tablespoons (60 ml) crumbled
blue cheese
2 *kaki* or fuyu persimmons, in
½-inch (1.25 cm) dice (replace
with apple if you prefer)
Salt
Pepper

EQUIPMENT

Salad bowl
Whisk (optional)
Measuring spoons
Knife for chopping and slicing

Method

1. In a salad bowl, mix or whisk honey, vinegar, and olive oil. Add the other ingredients and toss to coat. Adjust seasonings.
2. Serve with a baguette and some pâté for a complete lunch.

Pairing   Viognier

Roasted Garlic Artichoke (*Artichaut*)

*Yes, you can roast an artichoke. You will be
thrilled at the difference in flavor!*

INGREDIENTS

2 large artichokes
½ lemon, cut in half, plus
   ½ lemon, sliced into about
   4 thin slices
2 tablespoons (30 ml) olive oil plus
   more for drizzling
12 whole garlic cloves
4 sprigs rosemary
4 sprigs thyme
Salt
Pepper
½ cup (120 ml) aioli

EQUIPMENT

Knife
Baking dish
Foil

Method

1. Heat oven to 350°F (175°C).

2. Trim all but about 1 inch (25 mm) of the stem from each artichoke. Remove a layer of tough outer leaves. Cut about 1 inch (25 mm) off the top, and cut the artichokes in half, lengthwise. Scoop out the fuzzy choke and the tiny rough inner leaves with a spoon. This should all be done somewhat quickly and right before cooking as the artichokes will start to oxidize and turn brown immediately. Rinse the halves and use ¼ lemon to squeeze a bit of juice on the inside of each half to prevent browning. Wrap just the top part of the artichoke with foil to cover the leaves and keep them from drying out.

3. Spread about 2 tablespoons (30 ml) olive oil in the baking dish. Place 3 garlic cloves, a sprig of rosemary, a sprig of thyme, and one

lemon slice on each artichoke half. Season generously with salt and pepper and drizzle a little olive oil on each half.

4. Put the halves cut side down in the baking dish, trapping the herbs, garlic, and lemon underneath. Drizzle the leaf side with a little more olive oil and sprinkle with more salt.

5. Cover with foil or a pan lid and roast for about 45 minutes or until the heart is tender when pierced with a paring knife or fork.

6. When done, remove the now soft and delicious roasted garlic and mash it into your aioli. Squeeze the remaining ¼ lemon into the aioli and add a grind or two of black pepper. Stir with a fork to combine.

7. Serve the artichokes with garlic aioli for dipping.

Variations, Ideas, Suggestions These can be made earlier in the day and then reheated in foil before serving to guests. They can be served at room temperature.

Tartiflette

This is a relatively recent French "classic" from the Savoie region of France. It's caramelized cheesy goodness.

INGREDIENTS

2½ pounds (1.15 kg) potatoes, peeled
2 tablespoons (30 ml) butter
½ pound (225 g) *lardons* or bacon, diced
2 large shallots, cut into ½-inch (1.25 cm) chunks
½ cup (120 ml) dry white wine
½ cup (120 ml) heavy cream
Pinch of nutmeg
Pinch of finely chopped thyme
Salt
Pepper
1 garlic clove
1 pound (450 g) Reblochon or a similar cheese, like fontina or Port du Salut, sliced

EQUIPMENT

Knife for dicing and slicing
Measuring cups and spoons
Medium oven-proof baking dish
Medium pot
Vegetable peeler

Method

1. Preheat the oven to 350°F (175°C).
2. Boil the potatoes in a pot until just tender. Drain and remove potatoes from pot. When cool enough, cut into bite-sized pieces.
3. Sauté the potatoes in butter until just turning golden. Remove to a plate and set aside.
4. In the same pot, add the *lardons* and the shallot. Cook on medium-low for about 20 minutes, stirring now and then, until the *lardons* are golden and the shallots are caramelized.

5. Add the wine and let reduce until almost gone. Stir in cream, nutmeg, and thyme and remove from heat. Season to taste with salt and pepper.

6. In an ovenproof baking dish, rub a cut garlic clove over the sides and the bottom. Then scoop half of the potato mixture in the baking dish and layer with half of the cheese slices. Repeat with the other half of the potatoes and the cheese slices.

7. Bake in the oven for about 20 minutes until bubbling and golden.

Pairing   Pinot Gris or Sancerre

Variations, Ideas, Suggestions   Serve with a crispy green salad.

Oven-Roasted Haricots Verts or Asparagus (*Asperges*)

When people of my age group grew up, most of our mothers boiled or steamed vegetables. No wonder it was so difficult to persuade us to eat our veggies! They were usually limp and soggy, and the texture and lack of flavor were enough to put us off certain ones for life. Oven roasting was a game changer. This is the simplest method of cooking vegetables ever invented. If you have an oven, you're in business. Roasting enhances the flavor in vegetables, and the firmer texture adds interest to your meal. You can use this technique with almost any vegetable.

We were out recently with some friends who were enjoying the "what would be your last meal" conversation. The world-famous winemaker Justin Smith, creator of Saxum, said he would order a platter of roasted or grilled vegetables. We agreed that this is the thing we usually love best.

If this is just too simple for you, try the recipe for Hazelnut Orange Persillade (see page 208). It is perfect with either asparagus or haricots verts.

INGREDIENTS

1 pound (450 g) haricots verts or asparagus, woody ends snapped off
2 tablespoons (30 ml) olive oil
Salt
Pepper

EQUIPMENT

Baking pan or sheet
Measuring spoons

Method

1. Preheat oven to 380°F (195°C).
2. Toss vegetables in olive oil, salt, and pepper. Spread on a baking sheet in a single layer. Don't overcrowd.
3. Try either vegetable after 10 minutes, and if they are not done, check every additional 5 minutes until they are. The green beans will be done when they are softened but still have a bite. The asparagus will be done when they barely bend but are not limp.

Variations, Ideas, Suggestions If you don't have a reliable oven, cook the vegetables in boiling water until barely done, plunge them into cold water to stop the cooking, and dry them. Then pan roast them in olive oil, salt, and pepper.

Hazelnut Orange Persillade

—— SERVES 4 ——

Chopped fresh herbs add interest to almost every dish. You will find so many uses for this tangy mixture. Try it on potatoes, sprinkled on fish, or on broccoli for extra zip.

INGREDIENTS

1 garlic clove, crushed
1 tablespoon (15 g) chopped fresh tarragon
1 tablespoon (15 g) chopped fresh parsley
1 tablespoon (10 g) toasted and crushed hazelnuts
1 tablespoon (10 ml) grated orange zest
½ teaspoon (3 g) sea salt

EQUIPMENT

Knife for chopping
Measuring spoons

Method

1. Pile all the ingredients on a cutting board, and with a butcher's knife, chop everything together into a very fine crumb-type mixture.

Variations, Ideas, Suggestions

- Dangerous on roasted carrots or beets.
- Wonderful on trout or another roasted white fish.
- Super tasty on roasted or braised lamb.

Roasted Cauliflower (*Chou-Fleur*) with Currants and Capers

This cauliflower is so delicious that sometimes we make it to eat like popcorn when we're watching a movie on TV.

INGREDIENTS

3 tablespoons (45 g) dried currants
2 tablespoons (30 ml) Calvados or brandy
1 head cauliflower, cut into 1-inch (2.5 cm) florets (or smaller)
6 tablespoons (90 ml) melted butter
Salt
Pepper
3 tablespoons (45 g) capers, drained

EQUIPMENT

Knife for chopping
Measuring spoons

Method

1. Mix together the currants and the Calvados or brandy and set aside while you prep and cook the cauliflower.
2. Preheat the oven to 400°F (200°C). Toss the cauliflower with the melted butter, salt, and pepper. Roast until deeply golden brown, about 30 minutes (check it at 20 minutes). If not golden brown in 30 minutes, then cook a bit longer and check every 5 minutes.
3. Toss with the capers and the currants.

Variations, Ideas, Suggestions

- A perfect match with braised lamb shanks.
- Don't mix in the capers or currants, and eat it as a snack.

FRUITS (*Fruits*)

FIGS, PEACHES, PEARS, BERRIES, and other fruits are an important part of the French menu. For ordinary dinners at home, fruit is usually served as dessert. It also is an important feature of the breakfast table. Fruit, yogurt, and a piece of last night's baguette makes a dandy way to start today.

Cantaloupe (*Melon de Cavaillon*) with Bayonne Ham (*Jambon de Bayonne*) and Toasted Almonds

—— SERVES 4 ——

*Melon de Cavaillon is similar to cantaloupe
but a bit smaller and even juicier.*

INGREDIENTS

1 *melon de Cavaillon,* rind removed and cut into 1-inch (1.25 cm) wedges (or ½ melon, depending on the size)

6 slices *jambon de Bayonne,* roughly cut into ¼-inch (6 mm) ribbons

3 tablespoons (45 ml) balsamic reduction

1 tablespoon (15 ml) honey

4 tablespoons (60 g) roughly chopped basil leaves or 2 table-spoons (30 g) finely chopped mint leaves

4 tablespoons (60 g) roughly chopped toasted almonds

EQUIPMENT

Knife for slicing and chopping
Measuring spoons

Continued

Method

1. Arrange the melon slices on a platter.
2. Place the ribbons of *jambon* one-by-one on the melon.
3. Drizzle the balsamic and the honey on the melon and *jambon*.
   Scatter the basil and the toasted almonds.

Pairing Sancerre

Variations, Ideas, Suggestions

- Add a hunk of cheese from the *fromagerie* and a baguette and voilà!
  Instant picnic.
- For a vegetarian version, leave out the *jambon de Bayonne*. If you
  happen upon some gorgeous peaches or nectarines, you can substitute them for the melon.

Seared Persimmon (*Kaki*), with Fromage Blanc, Honey, and Truffle Salt

Our dear friend Ann made something similar to this for us one night and we swooned.

INGREDIENTS

4 ounces (112 g) *fromage blanc* (it's almost like ricotta)
½ tablespoon (8 ml) butter
2 firm *kaki* or fuyu persimmons, cut into six wedges each, seed core removed
4 tablespoons (60 ml) honey
Truffle salt or flaked sea salt

EQUIPMENT

Knife for cutting
Measuring spoons
Small sauté pan

Method

1. Divide *fromage blanc* onto four plates.
2. Heat butter in a sauté pan on high until bubbling. Sear persimmon slices for about a minute on each side, until they start to turn golden.
3. Spoon the persimmons on top of the *fromage blanc*. Drizzle with honey. Sprinkle with salt.

FRUIT AND VEGETABLE FESTIVALS

France is a country of celebration, so we are never surprised to find a food-related fête occurring somewhere in the country nearly every weekend. From small villages to large cities, people are bound to be using a fruit, meat, fish, or vegetable as a reason to gather, eat, drink, and have fun. Here are a few examples of the festivals you might enjoy.

Le Marché aux Truffes **(Truffle Market):** This festival is held roughly from November to March in towns and villages throughout Provence. A quick trip around the internet will give you specific information. You'll find truffle-scented oil (fantastic on pasta), truffle butter, truffle paste, and truffle/balsamic reductions that will enhance even the most ordinary plate of food. All of these will keep in the fridge for up to a year. Buying from the artisan not only supports this tiny industry but will save you a fortune compared to tracking down these products back home.

La Fête du Citron **(Lemon Festival):** Do not miss this world-famous weeklong festival in Menton, on the French Riviera, which has been held there from mid-February to early March since 1933. Up to 160,000 visitors flock to see the stunning procession of floats, gardens of lights, and other exhibitions. Local and international food specialties are a delight.

La Fête de la Fraise **(Strawberry Festival):** The town of Beau-lieu-sur-Dordogne claims to be at the heart of "Strawberry Country" and hence celebrates its Fête de la Fraise every spring. There are competitions for the best fruit, a massive strawberry tart, producers' stalls, music, and a parade.

La Fête de la Framboise **(Raspberry Festival):** Held on July 11th each year, this festival is in the tiny village of Concèze, which is in the Correze department of central France. The villagers come together to worship the fruit that has been growing there since the mid-1950s. You'll be amazed at the delicious products that can be made out of such a simple homegrown fruit. Visitors can lunch on raspberry-inspired dishes including granitas, wines, champagne cocktails, veal, duck, and snails cooked in raspberry vinegar, sweet liqueurs, tarts, coulis, and terrines while enjoying the traditional street entertainment and the picturesque scenery.

La Fête du Melon (Melon Festival): This festival is held each July in the town of Cavaillon, in Provence. The area's specialty is the Charentais, a small, round melon with a blue-green striped rind and deep orange flesh. Its aroma is irresistible. Melon tastings, fireworks displays, and a *pétanque* tournament are just a few of the attractions.

La Fête du Garlic (Garlic Fair): This celebrates the pungent bulb with wining, dining, and fun in the streets. After a September weekend of parades, a flea market, and a disco, the festival culminates in the election of the Garlic Queen, who reigns over the village of Arleux, in Nord-Pas-de-Calais, for the year.

La Fête du Apiaceae (Carrot Fair): Held in the Normandy town of Créances, this festival is on the second Saturday of August. The small town produces high-quality vegetables, carrots in particular, and every year the local farming community congregates to celebrate its terroir and the local produce with performances, a market, food stalls, and music.

La Fête du Mirabelle (Mirabelle Festival): The Lorraine capital region attracts thousands of visitors right after August 15th. There are concerts, balls, craft markets, and fireworks celebrating its favorite fruit—a small yellow plum. Miss Mirabelle is elected to reign for the year.

Cherry Beignet and Kirsch Fair: Cherry trees proliferate over the western slopes of the Vosges mountains, and every year the village of Fougerolles holds a festival to celebrate the incredibly delicious beignets (fried doughnuts) and the kirsch (fruit brandy) that the fruit produces (with a bit of expert help).

Oil and Truffle Fair: Held in Aix-en-Provence, what more delectable fare could you think of to celebrate at Christmas than olive oil and fresh truffles? The first pressing of the year's olives provides a sought-after virgin oil, which is sold alongside local truffles at this fair in Aix-en-Provence's Place de la Rotonde. Producers from all over the province exhibit their wares.

Chapter 10

DESSERT AND CHOCOLATE

(Dessert et Chocolat)

"Seize the moment.
Remember all those women
on the *Titanic* who
waved off the dessert cart."

———

ERMA BOMBECK

Recipes featured in this chapter:

*Apple (*Pomme*) and* Kouign-Amann *Pudding*
*Lemon (*Citron*) Mascarpone Mousse*
*Leftover Red Wine and Pomegranate (*Grenade*) Poached Pear (*Poire*)*
*Seared Banana (*Banane*) Crêpe with Hazelnuts, Brandy, and Petit Suisse*
*Raspberry (*Framboise*) Clafoutis*
*Chocolate Terrine (*Pavé au Chocolat*)*
*Hot Chocolate (*Chocolat Chaud*)*

DESSERT (*Dessert*)

Every day is a treat when I'm in France, but being allowed to ogle the outrageously beautiful baked goods displayed in a patisserie's window gives me a special thrill. My first visit to France was during my sophomore summer trip in 1960. I had never seen (nor have I ever seen elsewhere) such displays of artful baking. Delicate puff pastries—éclairs, petit fours, colorful macarons, and exquisite tarts—all decorated with precision and flair, demand almost as much careful inspection as the Monets and Gauguins do in the country's world-class museums. Many patisseries offer sandwiches and a place to sit while enjoying their delicious offerings, and there is always a bakery to be found in even the tiniest French village.

The signature French bakery items are croissants and macarons, which are imitated almost everywhere on earth, but never taste quite as they do in France. Every time I'm on an airplane returning from Europe I notice people lovingly placing their pastel bags of macarons from Ladurée or Fauchon in the safest spots they can find. And no wonder! They are fabulous and unique. Macarons are basically two perfectly smooth domed meringue cookies flavored and colored at the whim of the baker. The shell is crisp on the outside and melts in the mouth immediately. The filling, which can be sweet, tart, or savory, takes a leading role as you happily munch away. I was astonished when Tim came home one day and told me that McDonald's was selling macarons. Of course, he had sampled several and declared that they were pretty good.

One day Deborah and I were window shopping in Paris (that was the only way we *could* shop in the extremely upscale Saint-Germain-des-Prés neighborhood). We left the venerable, gorgeous Le Bon Marché, where we drooled over elegant, unaffordable designer duds and unique household items displayed in that exquisite confection of Victorian glass and iron.

Resisting temptation had made us hungry, so it was time to rest and enjoy something we could actually afford. I steered her to my favorite purveyor of macarons, Gerard Mulot, where it took us a long time to deliberate over dozens of elegant varieties. We made our choices and walked a few blocks to the Square Felix-Desruelles, a lovely little pocket garden honoring one of France's celebrated sculptors. We plopped down on a shady bench before a lovely bas-relief panel and tucked into our feast.

By this time, the two of us had polished off the entire bag of macarons and were fortified enough to enjoy a few more hours of drooling over all the beautiful things in that playground of the rich and famous. We topped off the afternoon with a glass of wine at Les Deux Magots and made another visit to M. Mulot's place to buy a treat for Tim.

Afternoons like that are what make France so irresistible to me. The atmosphere of unhurried appreciation for beautiful things, art, music, food, friends, and tradition invite visitors to slow down and emulate their hosts.

I find it fascinating that while the French produce some of the most gorgeous, sublime-tasting sweets in the world, as a rule, they are not overweight. I'm told by my French friends that those tempting treats that fill the cases of the patisseries are usually eaten only on special occasions. On ordinary nights in a French household, the desserts are nearly always fresh fruit. We try to emulate their self-control when we are in the country, but I must admit that we don't often succeed. Somehow a lemon tart or a chocolate profiterole manages to leap from a shop into Tim's cart on the way home from the farmers' market. See, everything in France is magical! The good news is that we walk so much when we are in France that we rarely add too much to our derrieres.

Deborah has developed some delicious desserts that may help you resist the offerings of your local bakery shop and satisfy your craving for a little sweet something after a meal.

CHOCOLATE (*Chocolat*)

The fantastic offerings you see every day in France's patisseries and restaurants are enough to make you never want to leave, but just as important are the chocolate emporiums. The French have a history with chocolate dating back to 1615; it was a gift to the 14-year-old King Louis XIII from his 14-year-old wife to be, Anne of Austria. More than a century later, Marie Antoinette brought her personal chocolatier to Versailles when she arrived in 1770 to become Louis XVI's queen. Let's hope she didn't take the poor fellow with her at the end of her reign! By the early twentieth century, chocolate shops were common in cities and towns throughout the country, and it was about then that people began to give chocolate as gifts for special occasions and as hostess gifts. Chocolate is so popular that the average French person eats 15 pounds a year. Once you have experienced really fine French chocolate you'll wonder why that number isn't higher.

Mass producers of chocolate use huge amounts of sugar to disguise the poor quality of their chocolate, while true chocolatiers use only pure chocolate made with cocoa butter, not palm oil or other subpar ingredients. The flavorings, herbs, spices, fruits, and cream are all top-quality, and instead of smashing their preparations into molds, their confections are dipped. This means the chocolate coating can be thinner and the finished product can be more dynamically flavored than their mass-produced cousins.

Chocolatiers are highly respected in France and the really fine stuff commands a hefty price. But if you're going to have a chocolate moment, shouldn't it involve a sublime, velvety, melt-in-your mouth experience rather than the gritty, sugary taste of an inferior product? There are chocolate shops throughout France, but of course, they aren't all of superior quality. So how's a civilian supposed to tell the difference? First, the shop itself, if it's a truly excellent one, should look it. The best chocolatiers' establishments are so beautifully designed that they resemble haute couture or jewelry stores. A kitschy store selling cheap chocolates and souvenirs is not where you will find the level of chocolate excellence that will give you the experience you're looking for. The very best shops are extremely simple but elegant, and when you enter you're sure to be intimidated by the wide range of choices and almost hushed atmosphere you'd expect in a first-class jewelry establishment. But you can rest easy: We've put together some suggestions to help you make the most of your visit.

To calm yourself, first just take a deep breath and let the fragrance of chocolate soothe your soul, then take a reconnaissance stroll around the store. You'll notice the *bonbon de chocolate,* which are bite-sized chocolates filled with a wide variety of flavors. There will be chocolate bars, which are rectangular. These may be plain, filled, flavored, or decorated with nuts or dried fruit. You'll see fruit dipped in chocolate and chocolate-covered marshmallows, plus dozens of other delicious creations.

As you peruse the divine offerings, be prepared for sticker shock. Like all good things, excellent, high quality, handmade chocolates are not cheap. A pound of excellent filled chocolates will set you back between 100 and 120€, and bonbons will cost you around 1€ each. You can satisfy your chocolate lust for around 5 to 10€ if you opt for chocolate bars. I know the price is shocking! But remember that these chocolates are so superior that you're bound to enjoy them more than some ordinary chocolate made with inferior ingredients. Plus, they're so satisfying that you'll be happy eating fewer.

Be sure to choose items with fillings, fruits, or nuts so that you'll get to experience the art of the maker. A plain piece or bar won't tell you very much about the expertise involved in producing such delicacies.

The unspoken rules are, like many traditions in France, subtle. If you want to fit in, resist the urge to handle everything you see. Chocolate is delicate, and the store will not be able to sell anything that's been even slightly damaged.

Since you'll make a significant investment in these goodies, treat them right to get the maximum enjoyment. Do *not* put chocolate in the refrigerator or you'll destroy its creamy texture. Keep it at cool room temperature. Although it's doubtful your purchases will not be gobbled up in short order, you should consume them within a week or two. If you want to keep them longer or take them home as gifts, you'll be wise to buy chocolate bars. They have a longer shelf life and aren't as delicate as the individual pieces.

There are hundreds of chocolate makers in France, but the *grand-mère* of them all is À la Mère de Famille at 35 Rue du Faubourg in the Montmarte district of Paris. Founded in 1761, it is the oldest chocolate store in Paris. Although there are several branches throughout the city and the country, a visit to the original building is a historical adventure. Imagine how many people have walked through that door to slake their urgent need for a chocolate fix.

Quality chocolate abounds in France. Two boutique chains have many locations throughout France. You're sure to enjoy both La Maison du Chocolat and Pralus, whose signature rich brioche is flavored with praline pieces. It's to die for! Also, the renowned chef Alain Ducasse operates many branches of chocolate shops bearing his name. Nowhere in France will you be far from a place to enjoy a rich chocolate treat.

HOT CHOCOLATE (*Chocolat Chaud*)

As with all of their food fixations, the French are fanatical and opinionated about their hot chocolate. You'll find it on menus in cafés, tea houses, chocolate shops, and restaurants everywhere. The debates about using water versus milk or cream for hot chocolate has been raging for centuries. Personally, we love the richest kind—with hot milk. It's just the ticket for a chilly afternoon pick-me-up. If you want to engage in some chitchat with a server, give some of these questions a go:

- *Est-ce un chocolat chaud traditionnel?* Is it a traditional hot chocolate?
- *Est-il preparé avec de l'eau ou du lait?* Is it prepared with water or milk? (Remember there is no right answer!)
- *Quelle est la teneur en cacao de votre chocolat?* What is the cocoa percentage of your chocolate?
- *Quel chocolat utilisez-vous?* What chocolate do you use?
- *Est-il servi avec de la crème?* Is it served with cream? (Viennois hot chocolate is always served with whipped cream and is usually a bit more expensive.)

‖ DESSERT (*Dessert*)

SINCE FRUIT is such an important part of the French dessert course, Deborah has created several knockout recipes featuring fruit. You'll want to make them all, and your family will be glad you did.

Apple (*Pomme*) and *Kouign-Amann* Pudding
—— SERVES 6 ——

Kouign amann is a pastry. Deborah has been obsessed with it since visiting a friend's new house in Saint-Malo. It's like a round dessert version of a croissant.

INGREDIENTS

4 tablespoons (60 ml) butter, plus more for the pan
1 tart apple, peeled, cored, and thinly sliced
4 cups of *kouign amann* cut into 1½-inch (40 mm) chunks
4 eggs
2 egg yolks
1¼ cups (300 ml) heavy cream, more if needed
1 cup (250 ml) milk, more if needed
⅓ cup (70 g) sugar
1 teaspoon (5 ml) vanilla
2 tablespoons (30 ml) Calvados
Salt
¼ teaspoon (1.5 g) each of suggested spices: cinnamon, nutmeg, coriander or others that you have on hand

EQUIPMENT

Baking dish (about 8 inches square/20 cm square)
Baking sheet
Knife for cutting
Measuring cups and spoons
Saucepan
Vegetable peeler or paring knife
Whisk

Method

1. Butter the baking dish.

2. Melt ¼ cup butter. Place the apple slices and *kouign amann* pieces on the baking sheet. Drizzle with melted butter and toss to coat. Toast in the oven until the *kouign amann* is just golden, about 20 minutes. Scrape it all into the baking dish.

3. Whisk together the eggs, yolks, cream, milk, sugar, vanilla, Calvados, salt, and spices. Pour over the apple mixture to cover. If you are slightly short on liquid, pour a little more cream or milk in. Let sit in the refrigerator overnight.

4. Bake in a preheated oven at 350°F (175°C) until golden brown on top, about 35 minutes.

Continued

Variations, Ideas, Suggestions

- This is wonderful with Chantilly cream, ice cream, or a drizzle of caramel.
- Try making it with croissants (about 5 of them) instead of *kouign amann*.
- You can also use cubed leftover baguette or brioche. Just cube it, toss it with butter, and toast it first.

Lemon (*Citron*) Mascarpone Mousse

—— SERVES 4 ——

This dessert is super simple and quite refreshing after a heavy meal. Adapted from a recipe by the venerable Mark Bittman.

INGREDIENTS

1½ to 2 lemons (preferably Meyer)
Lemon zest, for garnish
¼ cup (50 g) plus 2 tablespoons (25 g) sugar
1½ cups (375 ml) mascarpone
2 tablespoons (30 ml) cream or ¼ cup cream, unsweetened, whipped
1½ cups (200 g) fresh raspberries or blueberries, or any berries of your choice
3 tablespoons (30 ml) honey

EQUIPMENT

Bowl
Knife for cutting
Measuring cups and spoons
Whisk
Zester or fine grater

Method

1. Zest and then juice the lemons into a bowl (save some zest for garnish). Add the sugar and mascarpone. Whisk until smooth. Incorporate the bit of cream (or fold in the whipped cream).
2. Pour into 4 short glasses, martini glasses, or something similar. Cover and chill in the refrigerator.
3. Top with raspberries and honey.

Variations, Ideas, Suggestions

- If you don't have a zester, a microplane, or a fine cheese grater, don't worry. You can either grate your zest with any size grater or peel

Continued

the zest off with a vegetable peeler and then chop finely, hopefully with a sharp chef's knife. Or if you happen to have a *mezzaluna* (a curved, double-bladed chopper), which many French home kitchens have, you can use that by rocking it back and forth over the zest until it is pretty much pulverized. You could also put the peeled zest in a mortar and grind it with the pestle.

- You cannot substitute the mascarpone with cream cheese, no matter what the internet says.
- If you feel up to it, you can put this mousse in a cooked tart shell and pile the berries on.

Leftover Red Wine and Pomegranate (*Grenade*) Poached Pear (*Poire*)

So you thought you would finish that last bottle of wine that you opened a couple of nights ago, but no. There it still sits on the kitchen counter three-quarters full. You taste it and it's just not what it was. Don't pour it down the sink. Make this instead.

INGREDIENTS

½ orange, cut in two wedges
2 cups (475 ml) pomegranate juice
2 cups (475 ml) red wine
1½ cups (300 g) sugar
1 cinnamon stick*
2 cloves*
2 peppercorns*
½ star anise*
Pinch of salt
4 whole firm pears, peeled (do not remove stems)
¼ cup crème fraîche
2 tablespoons honey
¼ cup (75 g) crumbled blue cheese, room temperature
2 tablespoons toasted crushed pecans, walnuts, or hazelnuts

If you don't have any of the spices, you can substitute with something else or just omit them.

EQUIPMENT

Knife for slicing
Large pot
Measuring cups and spoons
Peeler
Slotted spoon
Small bowl

Continued

Method

1. In the pot, squeeze the two orange sections, throw in the squeezed sections, peel and all, then add the pomegranate juice, red wine, sugar, and spices. Bring the mixture to a simmer.

2. Add the pears to the pot and simmer for 20 to 30 minutes, occasionally turning with a fork or tongs until toothpick tender. Remove from the poaching liquid and set aside. Fish the solids out of the poaching liquid with a slotted spoon (or something similar) and discard. If necessary, return the liquid to the heat and simmer until thick and syrupy.

3. While the pear is cooking, combine the crème fraîche, honey, and blue cheese in the bowl.

4. Place pears on plates or in bowls. Pour syrup over and drizzle with crème fraîche mixture and sprinkle with the toasted nuts.

Variations, Ideas, Suggestions

- If the blue cheese doesn't appeal to you, whip together some mascarpone and orange zest, halve the pears and remove the core, scoop the mascarpone mixture into the pear, and drizzle with the sauce.

- If you are out and about and you find some candied nuts, substitute those for the plain nuts.

- This dessert is amazing with a scoop of great quality vanilla bean ice cream.

- You can poach your pears with white wine. If you do, forgo some of the stronger spices and throw in a vanilla bean or a cardamom pod. Skip the blue cheese and go for the ice cream with the sauce drizzled over.

- Of course you can also poach pears in brandy and honey, but that's another story altogether.

Seared Banana (*Banane*) Crêpe with Hazelnuts, Brandy, and Petit-Suisse

—— SERVES 4 ——

Use the leftover crêpes you might have purchased for other meals.

INGREDIENTS

4 crêpes
½ cup (120 g) Petit-Suisse
4 tablespoons (60 ml) butter
2 ripe but firm bananas, sliced
    into ¼-inch (6 mm) slices
Sea salt
2 tablespoons (30 ml) brandy
½ cup (100 g) brown sugar
¼ cup (60 ml) toasted and crushed
    hazelnuts

EQUIPMENT

Knife for slicing
Measuring cups and spoons
Medium to large sauté pan

Method

1. Lay out four crêpes on four plates. Divide Petit-Suisse between the four crêpes and smear down the middle.
2. In a sauté pan, heat butter over medium-high until bubbly. Add banana slices in a single layer (this is important; if they are piled together, they will not brown). Sauté about a minute and stir around a bit to brown the other side of bananas. Sprinkle with salt.
3. Deglaze with brandy and immediately sprinkle with brown sugar. Remove the pan from the heat.
4. Spoon the bananas over Petit-Suisse. Fold the two sides of the crêpes over bananas in the middle. Drizzle remaining pan sauce over crêpes and sprinkle with hazelnuts. Dig in!

Raspberry (*Framboise*) Clafoutis

—— SERVES 8 ——

A claufoutis is deceptively easy to make and wonderfully impressive to serve. It's basically a fluffy pancake with fruit, and when it comes out of the oven puffed up like a beautiful soufflé, everyone will think you're a genius. This dessert is traditionally made with cherries, but since pitting cherries, as you may have learned, can be tiresome, this version is with fresh raspberries. Deborah's friend Valerie, who lives in Bordeaux, gave us her recipe.

INGREDIENTS

3 large eggs
½ cup (70 g) flour or almond flour
1 teaspoon (5 ml) vanilla
2 tablespoons (30 ml) brandy or
    eau-de-vie, divided
1 teaspoon (5 ml) fresh lemon juice
¼ cup (50 g) plus 3 tablespoons
    (45 g) sugar, divided
3 tablespoons (45 ml) melted butter
¼ teaspoon (1.5 g) salt
1 cup (330 ml) whole milk
1 pound (450 g) fresh ripe rasp-
    berries or blackberries or mixed
    berries

EQUIPMENT

Baking dish, such as a pie plate
Knife for cutting and slicing
Measuring cups and spoons
Mixing bowl
Whisk (optional)

Method

1. Preheat the oven to 350°F (175°C).
2. In a bowl, whisk together the eggs, flour, vanilla, 1 tablespoon (15 ml) brandy, lemon juice, ¼ cup sugar, butter, salt, and milk. Whisk until smooth.

3. Pour into a buttered baking dish. Top with fruit and sprinkle with the 3 tablespoons sugar.
4. Bake until set, about 40 minutes.
5. Drizzle the remaining tablespoon brandy over the top (or even a little more if you want). Let cool just a bit and serve warm or at room temperature.

Variations, Ideas, Suggestions

- Test the custard with a toothpick. It's done when it comes out somewhat clean.
- Try substituting other stone fruits or berries, or a combination! You could even try figs.
- Serve warm or at room temperature. A great make-ahead dessert, it's perfect for a picnic and I've been known to eat it for breakfast.

Pairing   Raspberry eau-de-vie

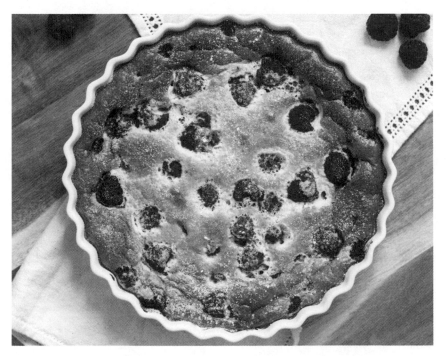

CHOCOLATE (*Chocolat*)

HERE'S A FITTING WAY to end this chapter. Chocolate, the king of sweets, is revered in France and almost everywhere else in the world. Be sure to try these two excellent recipes which are sure to assuage even the neediest sweet tooth.

Chocolate Terrine (*Pavé au Chocolat*)

—— SERVES 6 TO 8 ——

Pavé is the French term for a cobblestone or paver. When this dessert is made in a loaf pan and then sliced, it's shaped like a paving stone. If you put it in a cake pan and cut wedges, then you could call it a chocolate terrine. No matter what you call it, it's heavenly.

INGREDIENTS

2 pounds (1 kg) bittersweet chocolate, chopped
Pinch or two of salt
1 teaspoon (5 ml) vanilla
2 tablespoons (30 ml) butter
1½ cups (350 ml) rich red wine, such as Bordeaux
1 cup (250 ml) cream
¾ cup (100 g) shelled roasted pistachios, crushed (salt optional)
Raspberries for garnish

EQUIPMENT

Knife
Large mixing bowl
Loaf or cake pan
Measuring cups and spoons
Parchment paper or plastic wrap
Small saucepan
Whisk

Method

1. Line a loaf pan with parchment paper.
2. Put the chocolate pieces, salt, vanilla, and butter in a bowl.

3. Heat the wine and cream in a saucepan until hot but not boiling. Pour over the chocolate.

4. Let sit about 2 minutes, then whisk until smooth and shiny.

5. Pour half of the chocolate into the loaf pan, then neatly sprinkle the pistachios, creating a layer. Add the second layer of chocolate over the pistachios. Hit the pan on the countertop a couple times to remove bubbles and set the chocolate.

6. Chill overnight and slice to serve. When sliced, you should have a lovely green pistachio line through the middle.

7. Scatter raspberries to serve.

Variations, Ideas, Suggestions

- This dessert is lovely with macerated berries.
- If you don't have any fruit, sprinkle with a bit of sea salt when serving.

Hot Chocolate (*Chocolat Chaud*)

—— SERVES 4 ——

This recipe makes delicious, rich hot chocolate. Using high-quality chocolate is essential. And we would never make this with water. Don't be afraid to add the good salt—it really makes the chocolate flavor stand out. In fact, every dessert should have a little salt added to balance the sweetness and heighten the taste experience.

INGREDIENTS

2 cups (500 ml) whole milk
4.5 ounces (130 g) bittersweet chocolate, chopped (high quality)
Pinch or two of sea salt
1 tablespoon (15 g) brown sugar (optional)

EQUIPMENT

Knife for chopping
Measuring cups and spoons
Medium saucepan
Whisk

Continued

Method

1. In the saucepan, heat the milk until hot but not boiling.
2. Remove from the heat and whisk in the chopped chocolate, stirring until all the chocolate is incorporated.
3. Taste and stir in the salt and perhaps the brown sugar, if you think it's needed.
4. Swoon while you sip and wonder how you will ever go back to anything powdered again in your life.

Variations, Ideas, Suggestions Try topping with Chantilly cream (slightly sweetened whipped cream) or mix in any one of the following:

- Cayenne (or chipotle)
- Espresso powder
- Cinnamon
- Hazelnut liqueur
- A few drops of real vanilla extract
- Brandy (my favorite)
- A spoonful of caramel (Deborah's favorite)
- The tiniest piece of peppermint candy

WEIGHTS, MEASURES, AND TEMPERATURES

———

Converting from the American method of measuring to the metric system, which is used in France, can be confusing. The following charts should help you make the necessary adjustments. It's also important to note the difference between measuring liquid and dry ingredients. Fluids are measured by volume, while dry ingredients are measured by weight. To measure liquids, always use cups and spoons that are designed to measure liquids. Liquid measuring cups usually feature a spout for pouring. A dry measuring cup does not usually have a spout, and typically the lip is flat so that the cook can easily scrape off excess dry ingredients like flour or sugar.

Liquid Measurement Conversions

1 cup	8 fluid ounces	½ pint	237 ml
2 cups	16 fluid ounces	1 pint	474 ml
4 cups	32 fluid ounces	1 quart	946 ml
2 pints	32 fluid ounces	1 quart	946 ml
4 quarts	128 fluid ounces	1 gallon	3.784 liters
8 quarts	one peck		
4 pecks	one bushel		
Dash	less than ¼ teaspoon		

Dry Measurement Conversions

3 teaspoons	1 tablespoon	1/2 ounce	14 grams	
2 tablespoons	1/8 cup	1 ounce	28 grams	
4 tablespoons	1/4 cup	2 ounces	57 grams	
5 1/3 tablespoons	1/3 cup	2.5 ounces	71 grams	
8 tablespoons	1/2 cup	4 ounces	113 grams	1 stick butter
12 tablespoons	3/4 cup	6 ounces	.375 pound	170 grams
32 tablespoons	2 cups	16 ounces	1 pound	454 grams
64 tablespoons	4 cups	32 ounces	2 pounds	907 grams

To convert Fahrenheit to Celsius, subtract 32 from the Fahrenheit temperature, multiply that number by 5, and then divide that number by 9. To convert Celsius to Fahrenheit, multiply the Celsius temperature by 9, divide that number by 5, and then add 32. See the following table for some common temperature equivalents used in cooking and food storage.

Temperature Conversions

Description	Fahrenheit	Celsius	Gas Mark
Freezer Storage	0°F	–18°C	
Water Freezes	32°F	0°C	
Refrigerator Storage	40°F	4°C	
Room Temperature	68°F to 72°F	20°C to 22°C	
Lukewarm Water	95°F	35°C	
Poach Temperature	160°F to 180°F	70°C to 82°C	
Simmer Temperature	185°F to 205°F	85°C to 95°C	
Boil Temperature	212°F	100°C	
Very Cool Oven	225°F	110°C	1/4
Cool Oven	250°F	120°C	1/2
Very Low Oven	275°F	140°C	1

Low Oven	300°F	150°C	2
Moderately Low Oven	325°F	160°C	3
Moderate Oven	350°F	180°C	4
Moderately Hot Oven	375°F	190°C	5
Hot Oven	400°F to 425°F	200°C to 220°C	6 to 7
Very Hot Oven	450°F to 475°F	230°C to 240°C	8 to 9
Extremely Hot Oven	500°F	260°C	9+

ACKNOWLEDGMENTS

———

Un million de merci to Andie Talmud, Georges Maurel, Jeremy Schuster, Suzanne Flenard, and Nadine and Pierre Eid, our French connections who provided us with up-to-the-minute, local French information when we needed it most. Thanks to Tim Martin and Beezie Moore, who were always eager to taste test our creations. Thanks to Elise Moir and her entire family for enduring some of our failed experiments. Thanks to Dana Newman, our intrepid literary agent and mother hen, who once again sold a one-of-a-kind book; and to Róisín Cameron, who bought the book for Countryman Press and was a dream to work with. Thanks also to Diane Durrett for her thoughtful, thorough editing.

Special thanks to gifted author, editor, and cheerleader, Mark Chimsky, for his unwavering support. And a tip of the toque to our brilliant testing volunteers: Amy Butler, Jon Jaeger, JoAnn Cherry, Camille Cherry, Wendy Tuck, Chris Knowles, Molly Perello, Malia Baynham, and Alexandra Chamberlain.

REGIONAL FOODS OF FRANCE

1. PARIS AND ÎLE-DE-FRANCE

Paris and Île-de-France contain the most densely populated, wealthy communities in France. The political capital is also the hub of French cuisine. In Paris you will find ingredients from every corner of France as well as delicacies from almost all other food producing countries. It's a vast playground for all food lovers, and the number one tourist destination in the world. Although much of the arable land in the Île-de-France region is relegated to large industrial farming, Île-de-France is known for some outstanding locally grown products.

Look for these local products in stores and farmers' markets:

Wine and Other Libations (*Vin et Autre Libations*)
    Grand Marnier, exclusively made at Neauphle-le-Château and
        le Noyau de Poissy
    Local whiskey-spiked cider (*Cidre Briar*)

Cheese, Eggs, and Dairy (*Fromage, Ouefs, et Latier*)
    Brie from Meaux

Poultry (*Volaille*)

Houdan poultry is popular locally for its dark flesh and unusual taste. It's excellent in slow-cooked recipes.

Fish and Shellfish (*Poisson et Fruits de Mer*)

Crayfish and fish from rivers and canals.

Fruits and Vegetables (*Fruits et Legumes*)

Mushrooms (*Champignons de Paris*) grown in caves and old quarries; see Chèvre, Shallot (*Echalote*), Mushroom (*Champignon*), and Bacon (*Lardon*) Tartine on page 111.

Watercress from Méréville (*cresson de méréville*)

Faro apples *(pommes)*

Grolay pears from local orchards (*poires*); see Cherry (*Cerise*) Compote on page 87.

Montmorency cherries used for preserves and lamb (cerises); see Leftover Red Wine and Pomegranate (*Grenade*) Poached Pear (*Poire*) on page 231.

Desserts and Chocolates (*Desserts et Chocolat*)

Mille-Fuille—literally a thousand leaves; a divinely flakey pastry

Macarons—round, colorful pastries in a variety of flavors

Paris-Brest—pastry in the shape of a wheel, named for the historic Paris Brest-Paris bicycle race

Saint Honoré—named for the patron saint of pastry chefs, Saint Honoré is not cake-based, but a puff pastry confection

Galette des rois Parisienne—A wonderful Parisian and French tradition, this giant puff pasty has been eaten on January 6th to celebrate the Epiphany

Choux Chantilly—cream puffs

Brioche Nanterre—a delicious eggy breakfast bread named after the town where it was created. It is made by placing balls of dough on the baking pan and allowing them to rise during proofing and baking.

Brioche Parisienne—the classic brioche form. A large ball of dough is placed in a brioche tin and topped with a smaller ball.

Tarte Bourdaloue—a rich tarte, usually made with poached pears

Regional Specialties (*Spécialités Régionales*)
Rose Petal Jam (*Roseaux du Grand Morin*)

Regional Dishes (*Plats Régionaux*)
Croque Monsieur and *Croque Madame* sandwiches baked or fried boiled ham and cheese sandwich. *Croque Madame* is served with a fried egg.
Cuisses de Grenouilles—Frog Legs
Saucisson—Dry Sausage

2. NORTH-WEST (NORMANDY, BRITTANY, NORD-PAS-DE-CALAIS, PICARDY)

This area is known for all things apple—think cider, Calvados, and Tarte Tatin. Its Camembert cheese, mussels, and oysters give new meaning to a meal, and if you're into crêpes, you have just found your happy place!
Look for these local products in stores and farmers' markets:

Wine and Other Libations (*Vin et Autre Libations*)
Calvados—brandy made from apples
Breton Cider—traditionally served with crêpes

Cheese, Eggs, and Dairy (*Fromage, Ouefs, et Latier*)
Camembert—from Normandy, soft creamy cow's milk
Brillat-Savarin—made in Pays de Bray, cow's milk, extremely soft and creamy

Petit Suisse—made in Pays de Bray—lovely texture, mostly eaten for dessert or breakfast topped with something sweet; see Seared Banana (*Banane*) Crêpe with Hazelnuts, Brandy, and Petit Suisse on page 234.

Pont-l'Évêque—made in pays d'Auge from cow's milk, creamy and soft

Fish and Shellfish (*Poisson et Fruits de Mer*)

Try to visit Cancale, a town on Côte d'Emeraude.

Scallops (*coquille Saint-Jacques*); see Seared Scallops (*Coquilles Saint-Jacques*) with Peas (*Pois*), Bacon, and Mint (*Menthe*) on page 177.

Sole (*sole*)

Lobster (*Homard*); see Lobster (*Homard*) à l'Armoricaine on page 179.

Crayfish (*crevisse*)

Mussels (*moule*)

Oysters (*huîtres*); see Oysters (*Huîtres*) with Calvados, Apple Cider, and Brown Butter on page 41.

Fruits and Vegetables (*Fruits et Legumes*)

Cauliflower (*chou-fleur*); see Roasted Cauliflower (*Chou-Fleur*) with Currants and Capers on page 209.

Artichokes (*artichaut*); see Roasted Garlic Artichoke (*Artichaut*) on page 202.

Apples (*pomme*); see Apple (*Pomme*) and *Kouign-Amann* Pudding on page 226.

Persimmons (*kaki*); see Chopped Endive, Blue Cheese, Persimmon (*Kaki*), and Walnut Salad on page 200.

Regional Dishes (*Plats Régionaux*)

Galettes—rustic fruit tarts

Rich stews like *Cotriade*, a sensational marriage of bass, whiting,

mackerel, sardines, and other local seafood with potatoes and
onions

Claufoutis—a baked-custard fruit dish; see Raspberry (*Framboise*)
Clafoutis on page 236.

À l'Armoricaine sauce—a luscious tomato-based sauce

Far Breton—a prune-based dessert

3. CENTRAL (PAYS DE LA LOIRE, CENTRE, BURGUNDY)

In this area of France, the quality of the wine and beef have had a
major impact on its cuisine.

Dishes like *boeuf bourguignon* and *coq au vin* originated here. The
locals also take great pride in their ability to cook snails perfectly. It is
a legendary wine producing part of France.

Look for these local products in stores and farmers' markets:

Wine and Other Libations (*Vin et Autre Libations*)
Wine
Pinot Noir
Chardonnay
Beaujolais
Aligoté
Gamay
Sauvignon Blanc
Cabernet Franc
Chenin Blanc

Liquors
Guignolet (made from cherries)
Chartreuse (produced by monks)

Chambord
Crème de cassis

Cheese, Eggs, and Dairy (*Fromage, Ouefs, et Latier*)
Cheese
Chaource—soft cow's milk cheese from the village of Chaource
Epoisses—made in Auxois from cow milk, semi-soft, orange rind
Mâconnais—made in Mâcon from goat milk, soft interior
Crottin de Chavignol—made in Sancerre from goat milk, soft
flaky
Chèvre—goat cheese; see Chèvre, Shallot (*Echalote*), Mushroom
(*Champignon*), and Bacon (*Lardon*) Tartine on page 111.

Poultry (*Volaille*)
Géline fowl (*poule géline*)
Guinea fowl (*pintade*)
Pintade (*Guinea Fowl a la Normande*)
Poultry from Bresse

Meat (*Viande*)
Wild Game (*jeu sauvage*)
Lamb (*agneau*)
Charolais cattle (*Béail Charolais*)
Sausage (*saucisse*)

Fruits and Vegetables (*Fruits et Legumes*)
Pears
Strawberries (*fraises*)
Melons (*melons*); see Canteloupe (*Melon de Cavaillon*) with Bayonne
Ham (*Jambon de Bayonne*) and Toasted Almonds on page 211.
Belle Angevine Pears (*poires belle angevine*); see Crêpes with Pears
(*Poires*), Gruyère, and Thyme on page 43.

Cherries (*cerises*)

Currants (*groseilles*)

Mushrooms (*champignons*)

Fish and Shellfish (*Poisson et Fruits de Mer*)

Frog legs (*cuisses de grenouille*)

Pike (*brochet*)

Perch (*perch*)

Trout (*truit*)

Lake and stream fish (*poisson de lac et de ruisseau*)

Regional Specialties (*Spécialités Régionales*)

Vinegar from Orléans (*vinaigre d'Orléans*)

Dijon mustard (*moutarde de Dijon*)

Regional Dishes (*Plats Régionaux*)

Fish with white butter sauce (*beurre blanc*)

Boeuf bourguignon—a classic beef stew; see Beef (*Boeuf*) Bourguignon on page 151.

Escargot—Snails

Croûte aux morilles—a creamy soup served with crusts of fresh bread

Poulet à la comtoise—a rich chicken dish featuring eggs, cream, vegetables, and cheese

Smoked Meats

Salade Lyonnaise—a gorgeous salad made with lardons, frisée, a warm vinaigrette, and topped with a poached egg.

Gateau de ménage—a cake which is almost like a brioche, covered with an egg cream called *Gourmet*

Tartiflette—this dish, from Savoy in the Alps, is made with potatoes, *reblochon* cheese, lardons, and onions

4. SOUTH CENTRAL (LIMOSIN, POITOU-CHARENTES, TOULOUSE, QUERCY, AUVERGNE)

Toulouse, the capital of the region, is called the "pink city" because it is famous for its sausages. They are free from additives and preservatives, containing only pork meat, salt, and pepper. The area is also famous for the violets you'll see used for flavorings and crystallized in bonbons. Earthy, robust food is a favorite on menus in this part of France.

Look for these local products in stores and farmers' markets:

Wine and Other Libations (*Vin et Autre Libations*)
   Wine
   Vin de Branceilles
   Vin de Corrèze
   Vin de Pays Charentais (excellent with meat)
   Cote d'Auvergne from Auvergne
   Saint-Pourçain from Auvergne

   Spirits
   Cognac and brandy made from grapes (*Pineau des Charentes*)

Cheese, Eggs, and Dairy (*Fromage, Ouefs, et Latier*)
   Cantal—made in Auvergne from cow's milk, medium firm and
      slightly crumbly
   Fourme d'Ambert—made in Monts du Forez, cow's milk, creamy
      blue
   Chabichon du Poitou—made in Poitou from goat milk, dry flaky
      texture
   Roquefort—the famous blue
   Cabécou—sift goat cheese sprinkled with coarse black pepper and
      wrapped in two chestnut leaves
   Look for *Lescure* butter in Charentes. Local pastry chefs covet it;

see Anchovy Butter (*Beurre d'Anchois*) and Radishes (*Radis*) on page 94 and Avocado (*Avocat*), Radish (*Radis*), and Seaweed Butter Tartine on page 114.

Poultry (*Volaille*)

Challans Poultry—duck and black chicken are refined, distinctive poultry particularly appreciated by chefs

Goose (*oie*)

Duck (*canard*); see Pan-Roasted Duck Breast (*Magret de Canard*) with Seared Mirabelle Plums on page 125.

Meat (*Viande*)

Cattle from Parthnaise

Beef, lamb and game from Limosin

Dry sausages and *Saucisse* from Toulouse

Fish and Shellfish (*Poisson et Fruit de Mer*)

Oysters from the Olèron-Marennes basin

Mussels from the Bay of Aiguillon

Fruits and Vegetables (*Fruits et Legumes*)

Mushrooms (*champignon*s)

Haricot vert (*haricot vert*); see Oven-Roasted Haricots Verts or Asparagus (*Asperges*) on page 206.

Lentils (*lentilles*)

Regional Dishes (*Plats Régionaux*)

Cassoulet—a rich stew long-cooked with duck, sausage, beans, garlic, and herbs

5. EAST (RHÔNE-ALPES, FRANCHE-COMTÉ)

This part of France has taken much of its culinary traditions from German favorites, so pickled and pork-related dishes are popular. You'll find heavy, savory pastries and tarts, and of course Quiche Lorraine, which is the most famous dish in the region. Look for foie gras, jams and preserves during your stay.

Look for these local products in stores and farmers' markets:

Wine and Other Libations (*Vin et Autre Libations*)
   Wine
   Côte Rotie
   Condrieu
   Hermitage
   Chateauneuf-du-Pape
   Gigondas
   Vacqueyras
   Côtes du Rhône
   Vin Jaune
   Côte du Jura
   Trousseau
   Vin de Paille

Cheese, Eggs, and Dairy (*Fromage, Ouefs, et Latier*)
   Comté—cow's milk, especially firm
   Morbier—made in Franche-Comté, cow milk, firm with an interior stripe of ash
   Vacherine—made in Haute Doubs, cow milk, covered in pine bark which creates a slightly resinous note. Best served with a spoon.

Poultry (*Volaille*)
   Poultry from Bresse—reputed to be the world's best-tasting chicken
   Guinea Fowl (*pintade*)

Meat (*Viande*)
Sausages (*saucisses*)

Fruits and Vegetables (*Fruits et Legumes*)
Fruits
Young vegetables

Regional Dishes (*Plats Régionaux*)
Coq au vin—a classic French stewed chicken cooked in wine
Tartiflette—a potato dish from Savoy in the Alps; see Tartiflette
on page 204.

6. NORTH-EAST (LORRAINE, ALSACE, CHAMPAGNE)

This part of France is also heavily influenced by German food. Here, it's the staples that are best known. Potatoes, beetroots, and other vegetables that are harder to grow in warmer climates. You'll find excellent charcuterie, and best of all, the region produces Champagne.

Look for these local products in stores and farmers' markets:

Wine and Other Libations (*Vin et Autre Libations*)
Wine/Champagne
Côtes de Meuse
Côtes de Moselle
Gewürztraminer
Riesling
Sylvaner
Pinot Blanc
Pinot Noir
Tokay`

Beer
Alsatian Beer

Cheese, Eggs, and Dairy (*Fromage, Ouefs, et Latier*)
Bon dormois—a soft cow's milk cheese
Brie de meaux—made in Alsace-Lorraine
Bleu de Bresse- made in Bresse from cow milk, rich creamy blue
Munster—made in Alsace-Lorraine from cow milk, soft and
   aromatic
Carré de l'Est—soft ripened cheese

Meat (*Viande*)
Ham (*jambon*)
Charcuterie
Game (*jeu*)
Pork (*porc*); see Figs (*Figues*) with Crumbled Bacon, Chili, and
   Honey on page 39 and Pork Loin (*Longe de Porc*) with Apples
   (*Pommes*) and Onions on page 154.

Fruits and Vegetables (*Fruits et Legumes*)
Cabbage (*chou*)
Potatoes (*patates*)
Carrots (*carottes*); see Roasted Carrot (*Carotte*) Crudités with
   Yogurt-Tahini Crème on page 47.
Beets (*betteraves*)
Pears (*poires*); see Pear (*Poire*), Brie, and Thyme Tartine on page 110.
Raspberries (*framboises*)
Grapes (*raisins*); see Pickled Grapes on page 37.
Cherries (*cerises*)
Mirabelle Plums (*mirabelle*); see Pan-Roasted Duck Breast
   (*Magret de Canard*) with Seared Mirabelle Plums on page 125.

Apples (*pommes*); see Pont-l'Évêque and Apple (*Pomme*) Tartine on page 109.

Regional Dishes (*Plats Régionaux*)

Quiche Lorraine—cream, eggs, cheese baked in a flaky crust

Preserves

Alsation Flammekueche—a thin crust pizza with a *crème fraîche* and *fromage blanc*, topped with bacon, sliced onions and rosemary or scallions

Andouilette—a course-grained sausage made with pork; see Lentils (*Lentilles*) with Andouille and Vinaigrette on page 160.

Tarte aux Pommes—apple tart

Madeleines—light, buttery cookies, usually with a lemon flavor

7. SOUTH-EAST (PROVENCE AND CÔTES D'AZUR)

Spain and Basque cooking have influenced the food in this sun-drenched part of the country. Here you'll enjoy peppers, spicy sausage, flavorful tomatoes, and the famous Bayonne ham. Piperade (a mixture of peppers, onions, tomatoes, and eggs) is a local favorite.

Look for these local products in stores and farmers' markets:

Wine and Other Libations (*Vin et Autre Libations*)

Wine

Côtes de Provence

Coteaux d'Aix-in-Provence

Bandol

Spirits

Pastis

Cassis

Cheese, Eggs, and Dairy (*Fromage, Ouefs, et Latier*)

    Reblochon—made in Savoie, cow milk, soft and runny

    Tomme de Savoie—cow milk, semi- firm, rich and nutty, slightly sharp

    Beaufort—cow milk, firm and very rich

    Abondance—made in Haute Savoie, cow milk, firm

Poultry (*Voliaille*)

    Chicken (*poulet*)

Meat (*Viande*)

    Lamb (*agneau*); see Mead and Honey Braised Lamb Shanks (*Souris d'Agneau*) on page 156.

    Beef (*boeuf*)

    Sausage (*saucisse*)

Fish and Shellfish (*Poisson et Fruits de Mer*)

    Anchovies (*anchois*)

    All Seafood; see Seared Salmon (*Saumon*) with Fennel (*Fenouil*), Olives, and Orange on page 187.

Fruits and Vegetables (*Fruits et Legumes*)

    Olives (*olives*)

    Herbs (*herbes*)

    Lavender (*lavande*)

    Thyme (*thym*)

    Rosemary (*romarin*)

    Basil (*basilic*)

    Fennel (*fenouil*)

    Tarragon (*estragon*)

    Tomatoes (*tomate*); see Roasted Tomato (*Tomate*) Jam on page 45.

    Garlic (*ail*)

    Citrus Fruits

Regional Specialties (*Spécialités Régionales*)
Truffles (*truffes*)
Carmaque red rice
Olive oil

Regional Dishes (*Plats Régionaux*)
Bouillabaisse—French fish stew; see Simple Shellfish (*Fruits de Mer*) Bouillabaisse on page 181.
Poulet Provençal—chicken cooked with tomatoes, olives, and herbs
Salade niçoise—a hearty salad made with tuna, olives, capers, potatoes, green beans, hard-boiled eggs on a bed of leafy greens
Pan bagnat—the perfect picnic sandwich made with tuna, Niçoise olives, anchovies, and other deliciousness on a crusty baquette.
Ratatouille—seasonal vegetables cooked with olive oil and garlic

8. SOUTH-WEST (AQUITAINE, LANGUEDOC-ROUSSILLON, BORDEAUX, DORDOGNE)

This is a marvelous destination for those who love food. Its borders of the Atlantic, Spain, and the center of France give it almost unlimited possibilities for ingredients that inspire great cooking. You'll find substantial farm fair along with excellent seafood. There is definitely a Spanish influence.

Look for these local products in stores and farmers' markets:

Wine and Other Libations (*Vin et Autre Libations*)
Wine
Cohors
Bergerac
Languedoc-Roussillon

Corbières

Côtes du Roussillon

Côteaux du Languedoc

Bordeaux

Spirits

Armagnac—brandy made from grapes

Sauternes

Cheese, Eggs, and Dairy (*Fromage, Ouefs, et Latier*)

Sheep cheese

Roquefort—made in Rouergue, sheep's milk blue with creamy
texture

St. André—made in Rouergue, extra creamy cow's milk

Etorki—made in pays Basque, sheep milk, firm interior

Chèvre from Cevennes

Poultry (*Volaille*)

Free range turkeys (*dindes en liberté*)

Pigeon (*pigeon*)

Capon (*chapon*)

Goose (*oie*)

Duck (*canard*)

Meat (*Viande*)

Bayonne jambon—air dried salted ham

Jambon Cru—cured ham

Agneau de Pauillac—lamb; see Mead and Honey Braised Lamb
Shanks (*Souris d'Agneau*) on page 156.

Beef (*blonde d'Aquitaine*); see Hanger Steak (*Onglet*) with Sautéed
Mushrooms (*Cépes*), Cream, and Brandy on page 149.

Beef (*Boeuf de Chalose*)

Beef (*Boeuf Gras de Bazas, and Garonnaise*)

Fish and Shellfish (*Poisson et Fruits de Mer*)

Oysters (*huîtres*)

Mussels (*moules*)

Crab (*crabe*); see Crab (*Crabe*) and Poached Egg Tartine on page 92 and Crab (*Crabe*), Lamb's Lettuce (*Mâche*), and Avocado (*Avocat*) with Grapefruit (*Pamplemousse*) Vinaigrette on page 184.

Fruits and Vegetables (*Fruits et Legumes*)

Prunes (*pruneaux*)

Mushrooms (champignons)

Truffles (*truffes*)

Peppers (*poivrons*)

Tomatoes (*tomates*)

Chestnuts (*châtaignes*)

Berries (*baies*)

Honey (*meil*)

Regional Dishes (*Plats Régionaux*)

Confit de canard—duck in duck fat

Foie gras—a spread made with duck or goose liver

Pruneaux d'Agen—pitted prunes

Pâte—liver paste

Terrine—layers of chopped meat and vegetables cooked in an earthenware dish

Bourride—a fish stew thickened with egg yolks

Rouille de seiche—a cuttlefish stew

Catalan cuisine—food from part of Spain bordering France

INDEX